Lincoln Slept Here

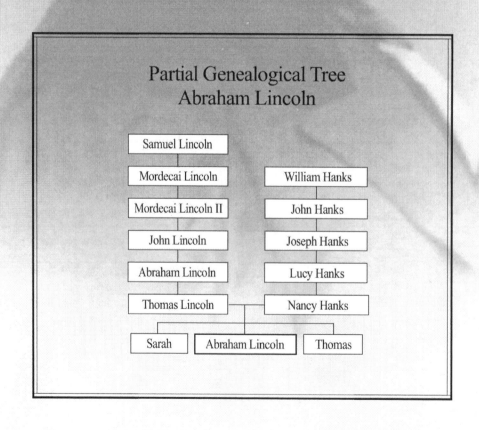

Partial Genealogical Tree
Abraham Lincoln

Samuel Lincoln

Mordecai Lincoln — William Hanks

Mordecai Lincoln II — John Hanks

John Lincoln — Joseph Hanks

Abraham Lincoln — Lucy Hanks

Thomas Lincoln — Nancy Hanks

Sarah — Abraham Lincoln — Thomas

Lincoln Slept Here

LINCOLN FAMILY SITES IN AMERICA

Abraham Lincoln's
Kentucky Years 1809-1816
Indiana Years 1816-1830

Edward Steers, Jr.

DESIGNED BY Kieran McAuliffe

DEDICATION

*This work is respectfully dedicated
to the National Park Service and its employees
in their 100th year of service
helping to preserve our history and heritage
and enriching the lives of all.
Thank you.*

Route of the
Lincoln Migration
from Kentucky
to Indiana

OHIO RIVER

The Indiana cabin.

INDIANA

Louisville

Present-day
Lincoln City
Gentryville
LITTLE PIGEON
CREEK FARM
Anderson
Creek
Evansville
Little Pigeon
Creek
Thompson's
Ferry
Troy
OHIO RIVER
Rockport
Cloverport
★ Fort Knox
Bardstown
MILL CREEK FARM
Harrodsburg
Owensboro
Pellville
Patesville
Hardinsburg
Elizabethtown
Springfield
Hodgenville
KNOB CREEK FARM
Danville
SINKING SPRING FARM

KENTUCKY

TENNESSEE

The Knob Creek cabin.

Lincoln Slept Here

ABRAHAM LINCOLN'S KENTUCKY AND INDIANA YEARS 1809-1830

Table of Contents

Rail Fence Bordering the Birthplace Property

Split rail fences became closely associated
with Abraham Lincoln as the result of a clever
stunt pulled off by his cousin, John Hanks.
At the Illinois Republican state convention in
Decatur in 1860, Hanks and future governor
Richard Oglesby carried two of Lincoln's split
rails from Thomas Lincoln's Decatur farm into
the convention along with a banner declaring
Lincoln as the "Rail Splitter" candidate.
The appellation stuck and Lincoln became
known as "The Rail Splitter."

PREFACE

Abraham Lincoln's second cousin Dennis Hanks, also the son of a Nancy Hanks (Lincoln's great-aunt), described his famous relative at the time of his birth: "He looked like just any other baby at first – like red cherry pulp squeezed dry. Abe was never much for looks." Dennis lived a few miles from the Lincoln farm at Sinking Spring with his foster parents, Thomas and Elizabeth Hanks Sparrow, and years later claimed to have run the two miles to the Lincoln cabin after learning of the birth. "I was the second man who touched Lincoln after his birth – a custom then in Kentucky of running to greet the newborn babe." Whether true or a product of Dennis's imagination in later life is not clear. Dennis had a great deal to say about his illustrious cousin and much of it requires some filtering. Nonetheless, he spent many years knowing Abraham Lincoln and even lived with the Lincolns for a period of time.

Like so much of Abraham Lincoln's early life, his birth was mired in myth. Among the many myths still celebrated to this day is Lincoln's "Melungeon" heritage. The term refers to a tri-racial group consisting of European, African, and Native American ancestry primarily associated with the Cumberland Gap and Appalachia. And not to be overlooked is Abraham Lincoln's Jewish ancestry. In 1865, Isaac Wise, a Rabbi from Cincinnati, wrote that "Abraham Lincoln believed himself to be bone of our bone and flesh of our flesh. He supposed himself to be of Hebrew parentage, he said so in my presence, and indeed he possessed the common features of the Hebrew race both in countenance and features." It seems clear that everyone wanted to pin his or her tail on Abraham Lincoln's donkey.

According to Lincoln historian and genealogist Louis A. Warren, as many as sixteen men shared the honor of having sired Abraham Lincoln, including such notables as Ben Hardin, governor of Kentucky, John C. Calhoun of Tennessee, Henry Clay (Lincoln's "Beau Ideal"), Patrick Henry ("Give me liberty or give me death"), and the grandson of Chief Justice John Marshall, Thomas Marshall. Rumors of Lincoln's "low-flung" birth began circulating within days of his nomination for the presidency. His birthright was fair game for his political opponents. Soon dismissed, or forgotten, they were resurrected by none other than Lincoln's close friend and law partner, William Herndon, shortly after Lincoln's death. In a letter to Lincoln's friend and law partner Ward Hill Lamon, Herndon wrote, "On further investigation, I now and have for years believed him [Abraham Lincoln] to be the son of [Abraham] Enloe." Herndon would eventually reverse himself, but the damage was done. The Enloe myth is the one that persists to this day and is celebrated by Enloe's modern-day descendants. In truth, there are actually four Enloes that Lincoln detractors put forward as his father, including Abraham Enloe of Rutherford County, North Carolina, which has led to modern efforts to erect a memorial in that county claiming it to be the birthplace of Abraham Lincoln. A recent essay on Lincoln boldly claims, "the North Carolina account of his birth is far more genuine and believable than the trumped up, government manufactured story fed the American public these past one hundred and fifty years." Boldly stated, but flatly false. The conclusions of all these alternative births are based entirely on traditional stories passed down over the years without any documentary proof from public records.

As with all such myths, the proof is in the pudding. There exist sufficient documents from tax rolls, marriage bonds, court cases, and public service records that refute all the claims of Lincoln's illegitimate birth. The numerous claims contain false dates, non-existent people, and confusion among existing people, not to mention malicious attempts to discredit Lincoln as our greatest president for political reasons. That Lincoln was the legitimate son of Thomas Lincoln and Nancy Hanks is easily documented. That he was born on the farm south of Hodgenville, Kentucky, is based on eyewitness reports by such as Dennis Hanks and Lincoln's claim that his father told him he was born on the farm near Nolin Creek, known as the Sinking Spring farm.

Not only are there sixteen men proffered as having fathered Lincoln, but also fifteen sites scattered in three states have claimed to be the place of his birth. Of the fifteen, eleven are in Kentucky. Places such as Thomas Lincoln's Mill Creek farm, Elizabethtown, the Plum Orchard farm, and Knob Creek have all entered claims at one time or another. The Sinking Spring farm continues to stand the test of research as the authentic birthplace.

Thomas Lincoln began his ownership of land at Mill Creek in 1803, where he established a home for his mother and sister and brother-in-law. Upon marrying Nancy Hanks in 1806, Thomas moved his young bride into Elizabethtown south of his Mill Creek farm. It was in the Elizabethtown cabin that Sarah Lincoln, Abraham's sister, was born in 1807. In 1808, Thomas Lincoln moved his wife and daughter five miles south of Elizabethtown to the cabin farm of George Brownfield, known as Plum Orchard farm. Here, amid the blossoming crab apples in May of that year, Abraham Lincoln was conceived. Nine months later he would enter life at the Sinking Spring farm three miles south of Hodgenville, Kentucky.

He looked like just any other baby at first – like red cherry pulp squeezed dry. Abe was never much for looks.

Dennis Hanks

Three children were born to Thomas and Nancy; one lies buried in the pioneer cemetery of George Redmon not far from the original Knob Creek cabin site. What we know of the Lincolns during this period of their history is gleaned from a paucity of land records, tax documents, and "traditions" drawn from neighbors and friends fifty years after the fact. While many myths and apocryphal stories abound, we can be sure that Abraham Lincoln was born on February 12, 1809, at the Sinking Spring farm, the legitimate son of Thomas and Nancy Hanks Lincoln.

When Lincoln was two years old, Thomas Lincoln moved his family a few miles to the northeast to the farm along Knob Creek. It was the last of Thomas Lincoln's Kentucky homes before pulling up stakes and heading northwest to Indiana. The Lincolns lived at Knob Creek for five years before succumbing to yet another case of faulty land surveys, forcing Thomas Lincoln to pull up stakes yet again and move: this time to Indiana. It was while living at the Knob Creek farm that Lincoln's brother, Thomas, was born, only to die within a few weeks. Tragedy would stalk Lincoln for much of his life, resulting in fostering a true feeling of compassion for the tragedy of others.

A view of the diorama of the Sinking Spring farm located in the Visitor Center at the Abraham Lincoln Birthplace National Historic Site.

Abraham Lincoln Birthplace Historic Site

*Entrance to the Lincoln Birthplace site
administered by the National Park Service.
Photograph 1985.*

Kentucky 1809-1811

The Birthplace: Sinking Spring

I was born Feb. 12, 1809 in then Hardin County, Kentucky, at a point within the now recently formed county of Larue, a mile, or a mile & a half from where Hodginsville [sic] now is. My parents being dead and my own memory not serving, I know of no means of identifying the precise location. It was on Nolin Creek.   Abraham Lincoln, letter to Thomas Hicks, 1860

Lincoln wrote modestly of his birth, for in truth, it was a modest event. In writing to the famous sculptor Thomas Hicks, Lincoln wrote, "I was born Feb. 12, 1809 in then Hardin County, Kentucky." Six months later he wrote to an old Kentucky neighbor and local historian, Samuel Haycraft, "As my parents have told me, I was born on Nolin, very much nearer Hodgin's-Mill [sic] than the Knob Creek place is." Unfortunately, Lincoln could not be more specific than to state he was "born on Nolin." Nolin was the name of a local creek that flowed near the Lincoln farm. Two miles east of the small village of Hodgenville the creek split, one branch flowing just to the north of the village, the other fork flowing south past the Lincoln farm.

The town square of Hodgenville, with the Weinman statue.

The birthplace farm was located three miles south of the small village of Hodgenville. The cabin sat on the high point of the knoll overlooking a natural spring, variously called the "Rock Spring" or "Sinking Spring."

Thomas Lincoln purchased three hundred acres (the final tract totalled three hundred and thirty-eight acres), known as the Sinking Spring farm, from Isaac Bush in 1808. He moved his wife Nancy and daughter Sarah from their temporary residence in a cabin located on the farm of George Brownfield called Plum Orchard to the new farm south of Hodgenville. It was here that Abraham Lincoln was born a year later on a cold Sunday morning in February. Ten-year-old Dennis Hanks, Lincoln's cousin, ran from his neighboring cabin to see the new baby: "I was the second man who touched Lincoln after his birth – a custom then in Ky of running to greet the newborn babe." Hanks later described the new baby: "he wuz the puniest, cryin'est little younster I ever saw."

The parents named their new baby boy Abraham after his paternal grandfather, Captain Abraham Lincoln. The name first entered the Lincoln lineage in 1686 with the son of Mordecai Lincoln and Sarah Jones Lincoln. The name came from Abraham Jones, the father of Sarah Jones Lincoln. The name stuck and appeared in each of the next six generations of Lincoln families.

Reports that Lincoln was born on the "wings of a blizzard" are apocryphal. Although it was a bitter cold day, there is no record of a blizzard. The day after Lincoln's birth was a normal court day for Hardin County and all five magistrates arrived at the courthouse, some having travelled over twenty miles. Also apocryphal are reports that an "old granny-woman," known as "Aunt Peggy Walters," served as midwife for Lincoln's birth. In the many years of Lincoln's life and presidency, no person ever stepped forward to claim such an honor, including Peggy

Walters, who was only twenty years old at the time of Lincoln's birth. The closest neighbors were Nancy's relatives, Thomas and Elizabeth Hanks Sparrow and Jesse and Polly Hanks Friend. Elizabeth and Polly were Nancy's aunts. According to Dennis Hanks, these people were the first to visit the Lincoln cabin where they found Nancy and her new baby and young daughter Sarah. No one else was reported to be present at the time.

Thomas Lincoln purchased the three-hundred-acre tract known as the Sinking Spring farm from Isaac Bush for two hundred dollars in cash. The farm was part of an original tract of thirty thousand acres that dated from 1786. In 1802, Richard Mather acquired fifteen thousand acres from the original tract and sold three hundred acres to David Vance. Mather held the deed, however, until the final payment had been made by Vance. Vance in turn sold his equity in the tract to Bush in 1805, who transferred his equity to Thomas Lincoln for two hundred dollars in 1808. While Lincoln acted in good faith, believing the property was free and clear, Vance had never paid off his debt to Mather, leaving the title to the property encumbered.

At the time of the purchase, Thomas Lincoln held as much as five hundred acres of land, including his property in Elizabethtown and the Mill Creek farm where his mother Bersheba and his sister and brother-in-law, Nancy and William Brumfield, still lived. The fact that Thomas paid cash for all three farms dispels the old myth that he was both a squatter and an indolent provider who could barely keep food on the table.

In 1811 Thomas Lincoln gave up the Sinking Spring farm as a result of the litigation over the money due Mather. He moved his family to a new farm on Knob Creek located a few miles northeast of Hodgenville, presumably using money obtained by selling his Mill Creek farm. In 1813, Mather brought foreclosure on the Sinking Spring farm for

Diorama in the Visitor Center depicting the birth of Abraham Lincoln.

the unpaid balance still due him by Vance. Since Vance had long since moved to Mississippi, Bush was ordered to pay Lincoln back his original two hundred dollar purchase price. Bush, however, failed to pay Lincoln the money, and the court sold the farm in 1816 at a sheriff's auction for $87.74, the balance due Mather. Thomas Lincoln lost the farm and his original two hundred dollar investment. By the time of the auction in 1816, Lincoln had moved his family to Indiana, determined to rid himself of both Kentucky's bad land titles and slavery, which his church had taken a strong stand against.

From the time Thomas Lincoln lost the Sinking Spring farm it passed through fifteen different owners before Robert J. Collier, publisher of *Collier's Weekly* magazine, purchased it in 1906. Collier turned the farm over to the Lincoln Farm Association in 1907, which held title until turning it over to the United States government in 1916. In all, twenty-three owners held title to the land that became famous as the birthplace of Abraham Lincoln. The current holding of the U.S. government of one hundred and ten and a half acres includes only one hundred acres of the original Thomas Lincoln tract of three hundred acres. But among the one hundred acres are all of the relevant sites associated with Abraham Lincoln's birth.

The fate of the birthplace cabin and the farm followed two separate courses. While ownership of the land is readily documented, the birth cabin lost its provenance sometime during the early years before Abraham Lincoln became a national figure. The farm passed through several owners between 1811 and 1867 when it was sold by its then owner John A. Davenport to Richard Creal. Davenport, however, claimed to have kept the cabin on his part of the original tract. Creal sold the farm in 1894 to Alfred W. Dennett. When Dennett purchased the farm from Creal he also purchased the log cabin from Davenport under the impression it was the original birthplace cabin. Dennett moved this cabin back to the birthplace farm on the crest of the hill where the Memorial Building at the birthplace site now stands.

The alleged birthplace cabin, under Dennett's ownership, then embarked on a series of tours around the country in an effort to raise money. Each time the cabin was moved it was dismantled and its one hundred and forty-three logs numbered to facilitate its rebuilding at the various exhibition sites. Unable to realize the fortune he imagined, Dennett sold the cabin to David Crear of New York, who stored the logs (or what was left of them) in a mansion on Long Island. In 1906, the Lincoln Farm Association purchased the logs from Crear and took them to Louisville, Kentucky, where they were stored until they were reassembled in the newly completed Memorial Building in 1911 as the "birthplace cabin of Abraham Lincoln."

The current Abraham Lincoln Birthplace National Historic Site consists of the Memorial Building that houses the cabin, the sinking spring, and the surviving stump of a large oak tree that served as a boundary marker for the farm. The Visitor Center located in the park contains exhibits pertaining to the site and the Lincoln family.

Diorama depicting the birthplace cabin as it appeared in its natural locale. Nancy Lincoln sits by the cabin door with her two young children, Abraham and Sarah, while Thomas Lincoln carries water from the sinking spring. Chicago Historical Society.

Thomas Lincoln's Three Kentucky Farms

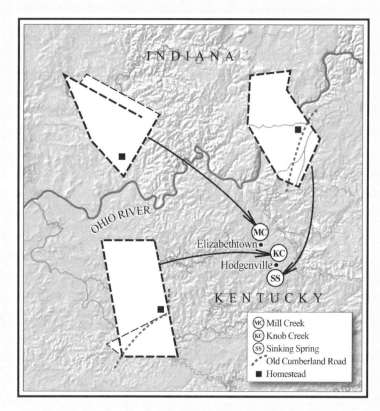

MC: *Thomas Lincoln purchased the 238-acre Mill Creek farm in 1803 while still single for 118 English pounds (the equivalent of $545). It was to this farm that Thomas brought his bride in 1806 before moving to the Elizabethtown cabin. He sold the farm to Charles Melton in 1814, consisting of only 200 acres, having lost 38 acres due to faulty land surveys.*

SS: *Thomas Lincoln purchased the 300-acre Sinking Spring Farm for $200 cash in 1808. The Memorial Park, maintained by the National Park Service, consists of approximately 100 acres of the original farm, including the site of the birth cabin and spring. Lincoln was forced to abandon the farm due to a faulty title, and the farm was sold at auction for $87.74. Although the court ruled that Lincoln receive his original sum of $200, he never collected the payment.*

KC: *Thomas Lincoln purchased 228 acres at Knob Creek and moved his young family there in 1811. The family lived on 30 acres of the 228-acre farm from 1811 to 1816, when Lincoln was once again plagued by faulty land titles, causing him to pull up stakes and head to Indiana where the Federal government produced land surveys that were true and guaranteed. Young Abraham Lincoln lived at Knob Creek from the time he was two and a half until he was nearly eight years old. In an 1860 letter he wrote, "My earliest recollection is of the Knob Creek place."*

After R. Gerald McMurtry.

An artist's rendition of Sinking Spring cabin. From a postcard.

Abraham Lincoln Birthplace National Historic Site

Flag Plaza leading up to the Memorial Building.

East side of the Memorial Building.

Path leading to the former Boundary Oak.

Abraham Lincoln
Birthplace National
Historic Site

Boardwalk leading to the nature path.

The Sinking Spring

Known variously as Sinking Spring, Rock Spring, and Cave Spring, Sinking Spring is the name generally used in early court records. The natural water spring is located at the bottom of the hill where the Lincoln cabin once stood and where the Memorial Building now stands. The names describe the natural features of the spring.

The water flows out of a small cave in the side of the hill and drops down into a collecting pool. The collected water disappears (or sinks) into an underground channel, making its way to the south fork of the Nolin River, hence the name, Sinking Spring.

Because of the necessity for having ready access to a good water supply, the Lincoln cabin was located close to the spring at the top of the hill. The cave was enclosed with stonework by the National Park Service soon after it acquired stewardship of the property and steps were added for easy access to the spring.

The cave, following its enclosure. Note pool at bottom center. 1990

The steps leading down to the cave. 1990

The cave as it originally appeared before it was enclosed with stonework, circa 1925. Illinois Central Railroad Company.

The Boundary Oak

The live tree, circa 1950. National Park Service.

The decaying trunk, 1981.

As early as 1805, the great white oak tree located on the birthplace site served as a survey marker for the Sinking Spring farm and its adjoining neighbors. The tree, estimated to be 28 years old at the time of Lincoln's birth, died in 1976 at the age of 195 years. It measured over sixteen feet in circumference (six feet in diameter) at a point six feet from the ground.
Its canopy spread covered an area of one hundred and fifteen feet.

All that remains of the last living link to Abraham Lincoln.

A cross section of the boundary tree on display in the Visitor Center.

The Lincoln Family Bible

The Lincoln family Bible survives to this day and is on display at the Abraham Lincoln Birthplace Visitor Center in Hodgenville, Kentucky. It passed through the descendants of Sarah Bush Johnston Lincoln who preserved it until its safe arrival in the National Park Service collection. This book served as Lincoln's first primer, and both its literary style and narratives became deeply ingrained in Lincoln. His speeches and writings are laced throughout with biblical references, and the simplicity and beauty of his writings are often biblical in structure. An example of Lincoln's reliance on the Bible is found in his Second Inaugural Address, which contains fourteen references to the deity and three direct quotations from the Bible. The family Bible also served as a record of the Lincoln family, listing the births, deaths, and marriages of certain family members. These records are in the hand of Abraham Lincoln. According to Carl Sandburg, during a visit with his stepmother at Goosenest Prairie, sometime after his father's death, Lincoln recorded certain genealogical information into the Bible. Part of the page containing the data on Thomas Lincoln and Nancy Hanks Lincoln is missing, torn from the surviving page. Dennis Hanks confessed to removing the record and keeping it, until it became so worn that it virtually disintegrated. According to Sandburg, Lincoln collector Oliver Barrett was able to show that this fragment taken by Dennis Hanks was copied by several members of Sarah Bush Johnston Lincoln's family into their respective Bibles, among them John D. Johnston, Lincoln's stepbrother. The missing fragment is alleged to contain the following inscription:

Thos. Lincoln was born Jan. the 6th A.D. 1778
and was married June 12th 1806 to Nancy Hanks who was born Feb. 5th 1784.
Sarah Lincoln Daughter of Thos. and ...
[Here the lost fragment is picked up by the surviving notation in the family Bible.]
Nancy Lincoln was born Feb. 10th 1807-
Abraham Lincoln Son of Thos. and Nancy
Lincoln was born Feb. 12th 1809-

Courtesy of Jared Frederick, Historymatters.biz

The Lincoln Farm Association

A certificate of membership issued by the Lincoln Farm Association in 1906 to raise money for the Lincoln birthplace park. The association raised nearly $385,000 toward establishing a park and memorial building. The certificate has the facsimile signatures of such notables as President William Howard Taft, Mark Twain, Ida M. Tarbell, Robert J. Collier, James Cardinal Gibbons, and Albert Shaw.

The idea to memorialize the birthplace of Abraham Lincoln began with a conversation between a young reporter, Richard Lloyd Jones, and his father, Jenkin Lloyd Jones, a Unitarian minister and admirer of Lincoln. The young Jones had visited the farm site and told his father about the deplorable condition of the farm. The Reverend Jones, who viewed the birthplace as "sacred ground," publicized the plight of the farm through his church publication, *Unity*, and when the farm came up for auction in 1906, convinced Robert J. Collier, the owner of *Collier's Weekly* magazine, to purchase the property. Collier bought the property for $3,600 and announced his intention of donating it to the United States government as a memorial to Abraham Lincoln. Collier, along with several prominent people, formed the Lincoln Farm Association to raise money to convert the property into a national park, complete with a memorial building to house the birthplace cabin. The Association membership grew to seventy thousand members and raised $385,000 through public subscription. The original cabin had long since been removed from the farm site and put on display in various places around the country. The logs eventually wound up in storage in a building on Long Island, New York, where Collier tracked them down. He purchased the logs for $1,000 and had them transported, accompanied by soldiers from the Kentucky Militia, to great fanfare, to the farm site near Hodgenville. The Memorial Building was designed by John Russell Pope and built by Norcross Brothers of Worcester, Massachusetts. A card index cabinet containing the names of those persons who made the purchase of the farm and improvements possible is located inside the Memorial Building. The cornerstone was laid on February 12, 1909, presided over by President Theodore Roosevelt. The dedication on November 9, 1911, was attended by President William Howard Taft, and the formal acceptance of the park on September 4, 1916, on behalf of the United States was by President Woodrow Wilson.

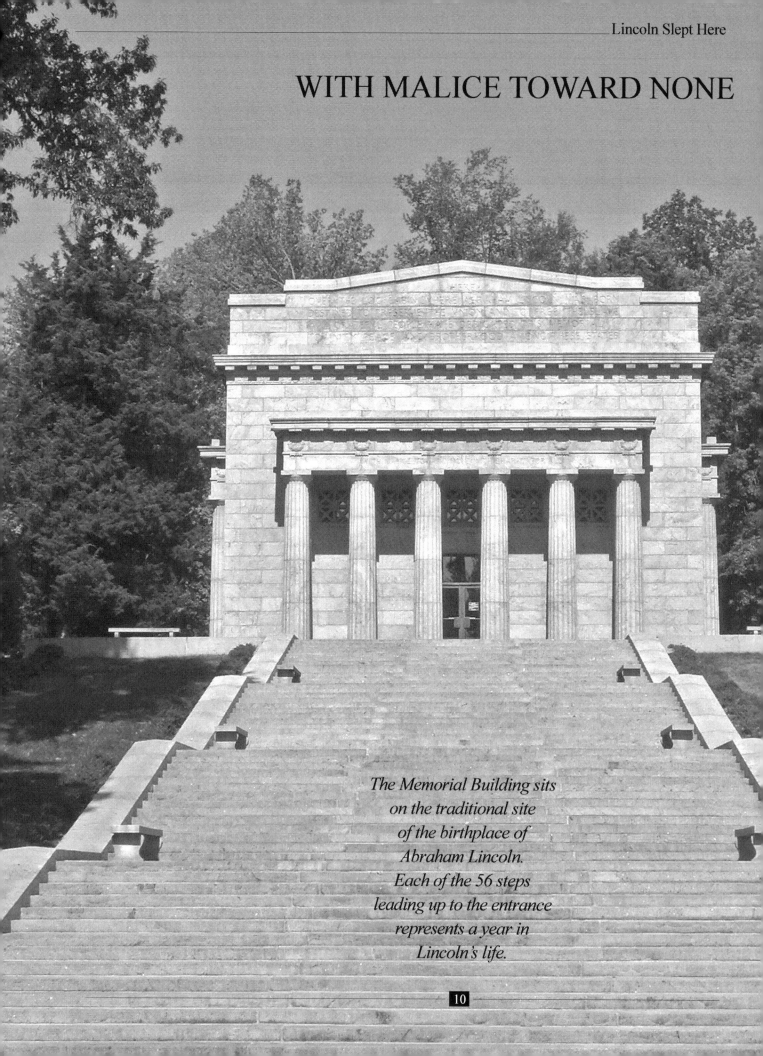

WITH MALICE TOWARD NONE

The Memorial Building sits on the traditional site of the birthplace of Abraham Lincoln. Each of the 56 steps leading up to the entrance represents a year in Lincoln's life.

10

WITH CHARITY FOR ALL

INSCRIPTIONS ON THE EXTERIOR
OF THE MEMORIAL BUILDING

LET US HAVE FAITH
THAT RIGHT MAKES MIGHT,
AND IN THAT FAITH LET US TO
THE END DARE TO DO OUR
DUTY AS WE UNDERSTAND IT
Cooper Institute, N.Y. Feb. 27, 1860

STAND WITH ANYBODY THAT
STANDS RIGHT
STAND WITH HIM WHILE HE
IS RIGHT, AND PART WITH HIM
WHEN HE GOES WRONG
Peoria, Ill., Oct. 16, 1854

HERE
OVER THE LOG CABIN WHERE ABRAHAM
LINCOLN WAS BORN DESTINED TO
PRESERVE THE UNION AND FREE THE SLAVE
A GRATEFUL PEOPLE HAVE DEDICATED
THIS MEMORIAL TO UNITY PEACE
AND BROTHERHOOD AMONG THESE STATES

THIS MEMORIAL
ERECTED
BY POPULAR SUBSCRIPTION
THROUGH THE
LINCOLN FARM ASSOCIATION

JOSEPH W. FOLK
President

ROBERT J. COLLIER
Vice President and Chairman
of the Executive Committee

CLARENCE H. MACKAY
Treasurer

RICHARD LLOYD JONES
Secretary

JOHN RUSSELL POPE
Architect

CORNERSTONE LAID BY
PRESIDENT ROOSEVELT
February 12, 1909

DEDICATED BY
PRESIDENT TAFT
November 9, 1911

BOARD OF TRUSTEES
OF THE
LINCOLN FARM ASSOCIATION

WILLIAM H. TAFT
JOSEPH W. FOLK
HORACE PORTER
CHARLES E. HUGHES
OSCAR S. STRAUS
JOHN A. JOHNSON
ALBERT SHAW
SAMUEL L. CLEMENS
CLARENCE H. MACKAY
NORMAN HAPGOOD
LYMAN J. GAGE
SAMUEL GOMPERS
AUGUST BELMONT
ROBERT J. COLLIER
AUGUSTUS E. WILSON
HENRY WATTERSON
JENKIN LLOYD JONES
THOMAS HASTINGS
IDA M. TARBELL
CHARLES A. TOWNE
RICHARD LLOYD JONES
CARDINAL GIBBONS
JOSEPH H. CHOATE
EDWARD M. SHEPARD
WILLIAM J. BRYAN
CHARLES E. MINER
WILLIAM T. JEROME
AUGUSTUS ST. GAUDENS

The Birthplace Cabin in the Memorial Building

Photo: Works Progress Administration.

The Birthplace Cabin

Fact or Fiction?

From a postcard, ca. 1950.

The structure now enshrined in the great marble building in Kentucky is a fraud when represented as the actual house. Robert Todd Lincoln, letter to Otto Wiecker, August 25, 1919

There has always been an acknowledgement on the part of Lincoln authors as well as the government agencies in charge of the memorial that positive identification of the cabin at this late date could not be established. However, this admission does not imply that it can be proven the cabin is spurious, and until such positive evidence is available it is unjust and almost sacrilegious to discredit this relic, which has brought impressive sensations to thousands of children, women and grown men as well. Louis A. Warren

Monuments and temples and statues have no emotion, no human sympathy, no voice. But here is Lincoln's old Kentucky home. Here is the log cabin where he was born. Here is a symbol of hope and cheer to every poor boy struggling against poverty for an honorable career. Remarks by Congressman Isaac R. Sherwood, (D, Ohio) in support of H.R. 8351 accepting title to the Lincoln Birthplace Farm, April 12, 1916

On April 16, 1916, the House of Representatives passed H.R. 8351 accepting a deed of gift from the Lincoln Farm Association for the homestead of Thomas Lincoln and the log cabin where his famous son was born. From the very beginning of its stewardship of the birthplace cabin, the National Park Service was faced with the problem of authenticating the logs as belonging to the actual cabin where Abraham Lincoln was born.

For the first fifty years after his death as many as fifteen sites rivalled one another for the distinction of being the birthplace of Abraham Lincoln. Lincoln, however, answered the question in a letter to Samuel Haycraft dated May 28, 1860, when he wrote: "I was born Feb. 12, 1809, near where Hogginsville [sic] now is, then in Hardin County."

Two weeks later he wrote a second letter in which he pinned down the location more precisely: "As my parents have told me, I was born on Nolin [Creek], very much

nearer Hodgin's-Mill [sic] than the Knob Creek place is." Approximately a mile and a half from Hodgen's Mill on Nolin Creek puts the birthplace site where it currently exists. With the location of the birthplace identified, the only question left hanging is whether the current memorial cabin is the actual birth cabin.

At the time of the dedication of the birthplace Memorial Building in 1911, a cabin of hewn logs, purported to be the actual birthplace cabin of Abraham Lincoln, was erected inside the Memorial Building. Did the logs used to construct the cabin come from the original Lincoln cabin or from another, unrelated source? The answer to this question has long been shrouded in confusion brought about by faulty research, wishful thinking, and simply a lack of records that bear directly on the question. Like the saga of Nancy Hanks's nativity, oral tradition in the form of statements given by "eye-witness" observers has colored the interpretation depending on who made the statements and when. On the one hand, affidavits of two individuals, one who lived on the farm shortly after Thomas Lincoln left it, the other by a reporter who visited the site in 1865, seem to confirm the claim that the cabin had been dismantled and the logs burned for firewood. Still other affidavits place the cabin at the site between the time of its alleged burning and 1865. And, if these conflicting claims are not enough to confuse the issue, there is the appearance of a set of logs purportedly taken from the cabin by an enterprising entrepreneur and his agent who went through a number of litigations and creditor law suits before the logs passed into the hands of the Lincoln Farm Association.

One thing seems certain; by 1865 the birthplace cabin was no longer standing on its original site. It was either destroyed, or fell into ruins, or was moved to another location not on the original farm. It is the latter possibility that gives hope to those who believe the current cabin to be authentic. The basic facts are these: After Thomas Lincoln moved to the Knob Creek property in 1811, the Sinking Spring farm passed through several owners before winding up in the possession of Richard Creal in 1867. Creal sold the farm to Alfred W. Dennett in 1894. When Dennett purchased the farm in 1894 the birth cabin was gone. It seems certain that the cabin was missing as early as 1860 when a local Republican state delegate visited the site and noted the absence of the cabin. In 1865, shortly after Lincoln's assassination, John B. Rowbotham, an artist, visited the farm site on assignment for a Cincinnati publishing firm for the purpose of making sketches of the cabin and relevant sites. In a letter dated June 24, 1865, Rowbotham wrote to Lincoln's law partner William H. Herndon telling of his visit. "It [the cabin site] is situated on a little knoll or rising ground & is now a barley field – Some rocks indicating the site of the chimney are still there. At the edge of the field are two old pear trees planted by Thomas Lincoln – between which – was a gateway leading to the house – Mr. Creal remembers him well – Near the spot is a very romantic spring from which the farm takes its name – & where no doubt Mr L as a child often strayed." Rowbotham seems to have found the spot where the cabin stood along with its famous spring, but no cabin. So, what is the structure currently located in the Memorial Building and where did it come from? The story of the traditional Lincoln birth cabin follows.

Shortly after Lincoln was elected president, Dr. George Rodman, a neighbor of the Lincoln farm property, bought an old cabin then standing on the birthplace farm and moved it to his property approximately one mile to the north. Eventually Rodman sold his farm and the cabin to John Davenport who proceeded to live in the cabin with his wife until selling it in 1895 to Alfred Dennett, the new owner of the Lincoln farm. Dennett moved the cabin back near the original cabin site on the Lincoln farm. It wasn't on its new site long before the cabin was disassembled and the logs shipped to Nash-

ville, Tennessee, for its Centennial celebration in 1897. After suffering through several more exhibitions and expositions, the cabin was disassembled one last time and placed in storage on Long Island, New York.

Dennett, a would-be entrepreneur suffering under financial difficulties, conveyed the cabin along with the farm to David Crear in February 1899 in lieu of a debt he owed to Crear. The transaction between Dennett and Crear is murky, since Dennett still acted as if he owned the property and was trying to convince the United States government to buy the cabin. Dennett filed for bankruptcy in 1901, claiming his only assets were "clothing" valued at $20. Dennett then filed suit against Crear to regain title to the farm that Crear now owned. The Larue County Circuit Court ruled that the original conveyance from Dennett to Crear was fraudulent and ordered the farm (and cabin) be sold by a commissioner of the court. On Monday, August 28, 1905, the properties were put up for auction and purchased by Robert J. Collier of *Collier's Weekly* magazine for $3,600. Crear, however, retained possession of the logs that were still in storage in a building on Long Island. Crear retained control of the logs when Dennett was declared insane and committed to a State Hospital in California in 1904. Collier then purchased the logs from Crear in 1906 for $1,000 and turned the entire package, farm and logs, over to the Lincoln Farm Association.

The next phase of the story involved authenticating the logs. What is missing from the story up to this point is the fact that when Dennett originally went on tour with the Lincoln logs, he and his agent, James W. Bigham, had also taken along a log cabin that they claimed to be the birthplace of Jefferson Davis. As the two cabins moved from show to show, being disassembled and reassembled, the logs became mixed and went into storage together in New York. Apparently at this time, the mixing was such that it was impossible to tell all of the logs apart. Since no interest was shown in the Davis cabin, the combined set of logs was shipped to Louisville, Kentucky, for eventual assembly in the Memorial Building as the cabin of Lincoln's birth.

The Lincoln Farm Association, concerned over the

The "Abraham Lincoln-Jefferson Davis" cabin during its erection in Louisville, Kentucky. Following the display of the two alleged cabins at the Nashville Centennial Exposition in 1897, the logs became mixed. Logs from the two cabins were used to construct the cabin pictured above. Louisville *Courier-Journal,* June 15, 1906.

Part of the broadside announcing the court-ordered sale of the Lincoln birthplace farm. The farm sold for $87.74. Author's collection.

The Lincoln logs in the process of being transferred from their storage building on Long Island to the birthplace farm in Kentucky, 1906. Library of Congress.

cabin's authenticity, obtained three affidavits attesting to the origin of the logs. John Davenport attested to having moved into the cabin on his property in 1875 – the same cabin he sold to Alfred Dennett in 1895 who removed the logs back to the Lincoln site the same year. A second affidavit, by Mrs. Zerelda Jane Goff, who was born in 1820 and lived near the Lincoln farm, stated that a family named Skaggs lived in the old Lincoln cabin and that a man by the name of Lafayette Wilson had hauled the logs for George Rodman to his farm in 1860. The third affidavit was ascribed to by Lafayette Wilson who claimed he was hired to move the logs by a man named Daniel Dyer, and he moved them in March of 1860 to the farm later occupied by John Davenport. No mention was made of George Rodman in Wilson's affidavit.

These affidavits, despite their conflicting claims, were submitted to a commission of four historians, who after reviewing them declared the logs authentic. In 1911, the Lincoln Memorial Building, complete with the Rodman-Davenport-Dennett log cabin, was dedicated and the cabin marched into history and the hearts of the American people. But not all the American people made a place for the cabin in their hearts. Robert Todd Lincoln, the president's son, wrote to Otto Wiecker of New York in 1919 stating that "The structure enshrined in a great marble building in Kentucky is a fraud when represented as the actual house." And, indeed, there are problems with the cabin's authenticity.

In 1948, Roy Hays, an insurance investigator from Grosse Pointe Park, Michigan, with a passion for research, wrote an article for the Abraham Lincoln Association in which he presented his own findings on the cabin's authenticity. Hays concluded that the cabin was not authentic and merely represented a "traditional cabin" cleverly promoted by a would-be entrepreneur. Balancing Hays's position was that of Louis A. Warren who wrote a series of articles on the cabin that he published in *Lincoln Lore*. These two scholars uncovered and discussed all the relevant data that existed to date on the question of the cabin's authenticity. The sum of the two arguments follows.

Hays's conclusion was based primarily on the interviews of two individuals intimately associated with the birthplace site during contemporary times. Jacob S. Brothers (born 1819) gave an interview in 1899 and again in 1903 in which he stated, "In the year 1827 when I was eight years old, my father purchased the old farm on which Abraham Lincoln was born. We lived in the house in which Lincoln was born. After some years, my father built another house almost like the first house [Lincoln birthplace cabin]. The old house was torn down, and to my knowledge, the logs were burned for firewood. Later he built a hewed log house. The pictures we often see of the house in which Lincoln was born are the pictures of the first house built by my father." These statements by Brothers have come to form the basis for those who claim the current cabin is not authentic but rather a replacement produced by John Davenport in 1895 and eventually acquired by the Lincoln Farm Association (through Robert J. Collier) in 1906.

There are several things troublesome about Brothers's statements. First, his father did not own the Lincoln farm in 1827; he purchased it in 1835, eight years later. He lived on the farm for only five years, from 1835 until 1840. In 1840 he was evicted for failure to pay the purchase price. Brothers failed to defend his eviction when he did not pay the $20 necessary to defend the suit. Jacob Brothers would have been sixteen years old at the time, not eight. Wherever Jacob Brothers lived in 1827 at the age of eight, it could not have been the Lincoln cabin. According to Brothers, his father built two cabins in the five-year span, the second one "hewed." There are two points troubling here. First,

Robert Todd Lincoln
Library of Congress

it implies that the first two cabins were not "hewed", but "round", and second, it represents an unusual amount of cabin building within a period of five years – especially for a family that was evicted for failure to pay its mortgage. And last, Brothers's statement about the "pictures we often see of the house in which Lincoln was born are the pictures of the first house built by my father" certainly refers to the photograph by Russell T. Evans taken in 1895. This photograph is of the John Davenport cabin that went on the road only to have its logs mixed with the Jefferson Davis logs before becoming the "traditional" Lincoln birthplace cabin. The implication that Brothers gave in his affidavit is inconsistent with the photograph of a "hewed" cabin. Brothers stated that the cabin in the photograph is the "first house built by my father." But according to Brothers own affidavit, the first house built by his father was made of "round" logs, not hewed ones. It was the second cabin that was made of "hewed" logs. Brothers was eighty-four years old at the time of his affidavit and was recalling events that occurred seventy-six years before. The inconsistencies in his statements cast serious doubt on their reliability as to the Lincoln cabin and its authenticity.

The second point developed by Hays in arriving at his conclusion about the cabin's authenticity was in the statement by John B. Rowbotham. Rowbotham was an artist, and as Hays said, a "keen observer." In 1865 he journeyed to the site of the birthplace specifically to sketch the cabin. He could not find it. In the letter to William H. Herndon on June 24, 1865, Rowbotham wrote: "...from E. T. [Elizabethtown] proceed[ed] to Hodgenville which is about ten miles south east of there – & inquire[d] the way to Rock Spring farm [also known as the Sinking Spring farm] owned by Mr. R. A. Creal, better known as 'old Dickey Creal' – The farm is about 3 miles south east of Hodgenville & a good straight road – The site of Mr. L's birthplace is on this farm about five hundred yards from Mr. Creals house." Clearly, the cabin

was gone when Rowbotham visited the site in 1865.

The last problem that Hays considered was the statement by Dennett's partner James W. Bigham that the cabin had been bought by Dr. George Rodman from Richard Creal following Rodman's return from Washington in 1861 where he had an interview with Lincoln. On his return, Rodman moved the logs to his farm a mile away. Rodman eventually sold his farm and the log cabin to Davenport and the rest was history. Unfortunately, it was Dr. Jesse Rodman who visited Lincoln in 1861 and not his brother George. It is just such inconsistencies that cause researchers so much trouble in attempting to find out the facts when dealing with oral tradition. While the Hays study raises serious questions regarding the cabin's authenticity, it raises as many questions as it appears to answer.

In his own studies supporting the authenticity of the cabin, Louis A. Warren uncovered statements that also bear on the question. Warren uncovered a letter written by a soldier in the 19th Illinois Infantry describing his visit to the farm in the fall of 1861: "I was then acting as a scout and was sent to where he [Lincoln] was born. I hunted up the owner of the place; he was living on the place but not in the same cabin. I asked him if he was shure [sic] this was the cabin where the President was born. He said he was. ... There had been no window in the house and he had put a half sash window and had put flat rocks under some posts when there [sic] bottoms had rotted. Looking from the door to the left end was the fireplace, which took up ½ of the end. It was made of rocks and clay about 7 feet and split sticks and clay the rest of the way up. On the right at far side of

Louis A. Warren
Stedman Studios, Fort Wayne, Ind.

A replica of the birthplace cabin on display at the Chicago World's Fair in 1933. From a postcard. Gerson Brothers, Chicago, Illinois.

The cabin in this picture is a replica cabin, ca. 1909. From a stereographic view by the Keystone View Company.

the room was the bedstead. ... The stairway was a pole with 1 and a ½ inch augur holes and wooden pins drove through about a foot on each side of the pole. Some flat stones were sunk level with the ground in front of the fireplace was all – the door was made of split boards with wooden hinges and a wooden latch."

Warren also reported two other accounts that added to the oral tradition. A Larue County correspondent wrote in the *Missouri Telegraph* on November 23, 1860, "The Lincoln farm is old and well worn. In an old field near a running brook the ruins of a pioneer cabin are pointed out as the birthplace of the President-elect." The second account is from another soldier, Robert Harvey, who wrote in the Nebraska State Journal on February 11, 1909, "I saw the rude log cabin in which Lincoln was born, in October, 1862. It was a few days after the battle of Perryville, Kentucky, when in the early afternoon we approached a low one-story cabin on our left. A rail fence ran along in front and on one corner was stuck a cracker box lid on which was chalked, 'Birthplace of President Lincoln.' The chimney was at the end of the building we were approaching, and was built of splints or sticks and daubed with mud. The roof was of clapboards and held in place by poles laid lengthwise. ... There was a door and a square window on the side facing the road and some of the logs had the appearance of being much decayed. A pear tree stood at the farther end of the building, but its uninviting fruit remained unmolested."

If we are to believe the above, it seems clear that there was a cabin on the site as late as 1862 and that it was gone by 1865. Where it had gone is not clear, although the proponents of the cabin's authenticity would say that it had gone to the John Davenport farm and from there to the Lincoln Farm Association, ending up in the Memorial Building. The National Park Service, which administers the Birthplace Site, has never represented the cabin as authentic. It does refer to the cabin as "traditional."

Oral tradition by its very nature is hearsay in character. Neither the statements presented by Warren nor by Hays answer conclusively the question concerning the traditional cabin's authenticity. What is clear from Hays's

research is that the logs, which make up the cabin housed in the Memorial, are mixed, coming from two cabins as they toured the east.

Finally, in 2004, the National Park Service supported a "tree-ring" analysis (dendrochronological analysis) on select logs from the cabin. By analyzing the tree rings from these select samples, investigators dated the logs to the 1840s and 1850s. Caution should apply, however, as these select samples may represent a few replacement logs resulting from the shuffling and mingling of the logs over the years. Perhaps impracticable, but a sampling of all of the logs would be more definitive. The weight of evidence, however, is against the authenticity of the cabin.

The cabin that now sits in the Memorial Building is the cabin that Dennett and Bigham took on tour. It is a cabin the two men built from logs taken from another cabin and foisted on the American people as a hoax. What is evident, however, is that the Lincoln birthplace site, including the cabin, represents a shrine that symbolizes the birthplace of our greatest president. It is a place where we can come and reflect on his origins and great life and the heritage of our nation. Congressman Isaac Sherwood presciently referred to the log cabin in 1916 as a symbol, one that all Americans can look to as a testament to American democracy.

Dwight Pitcaithley, former Chief Historian for the National Park Service and former president of the National Council for Public History, put it best when he wrote: "Our collective heritage is as much memory as fact, as much myth as reality, as much perception as preservation. The public's perception of the Lincoln cabin is important to the nation's image and an indispensable part of the nation's ritualistic public tribute to its own humble origins. It is symbolic of a need for an accessible past and a willingness to embrace myths that are too popular, too powerful, to be diminished by the truth."

When the cabin was placed in the Memorial Building, its size was too large for the space provided. Visitor circulation was difficult. The cabin was reduced from 16x18 feet to 12x17 feet. The pieces removed from the ends of the logs were donated to the Ladies Lincoln League of Hodgenville and cut into pieces sold to raise money for the local Library Fund.

An Historian and Deltiologist's Dream

An abundance of Lincoln postcards rank first among collectibles. In his comprehensive catalogue of Lincoln postcards, James L. Lowe lists over nine hundred different cards pertaining to every aspect of Abraham Lincoln's life and death. Among the more popular and numerous examples are depictions of the birth cabin. To the historian, postcards can be a valuable resource as they often depict rare images or scenes no longer extant. In some instances, postcards are the only source of information about sites long gone. Below is a sampling of twentieth century postcards depicting the birth cabin.

Signs of Lincoln on the Land:
the commercialization of Abraham Lincoln.

A few of the many business signs that dot the landscape in and around Hodgenville.

Adolph Weinman's heroic bronze statue of Lincoln located in the town square in Hodgenville, Kentucky. Dedicated May 31, 1909.

The Knob Creek Cabin

The cabin, located at the Abraham Lincoln Boyhood Home at Knob Creek, although not the cabin the Lincoln family lived in, is believed to be a cabin of the period (1811-1816). It is alleged to have been reconstructed in 1931 from the logs of the Austin Gollaher family cabin that was located not far from the Lincoln cabin. The logs are joined together at the corners by a method of overlap that secures them in place by notching, according to a pattern known as "the Kentucky notch." The style of notching was so popular among the early Kentucky pioneers that it can be found as far away as Thomas Lincoln's cabin at Goosenest Prairie near Charleston, Illinois.

Kentucky 1811-1816

Knob Creek: The Boyhood Home

Here little Abe grew out of one shirt into another.
Carl Sandburg

My earliest recollection is of the Knob Creek place.
Abraham Lincoln

The new farm was located approximately seven miles northeast of the village of Hodgenville, which placed it ten miles from the birthplace near Nolin Creek. But as with the farm on Nolin Creek, Hodgenville was still the center of commerce for the Lincoln family. Situated on one of the area's principal knobs, the farm proved considerably superior to the Nolin Creek farm, with richer soil.

The great Lincoln biographer Carl Sandburg told the story of young Abraham Lincoln's boyhood years on the Knob Creek farm in his epic biography, *The Prairie Years:*

> On the Knob Creek farm the child Abraham Lincoln learned to talk, to form words with his tongue and the roof of his mouth and the force of his breath from lungs and throat… Abe was the chore-boy of the Knob Creek farm as soon as he grew big enough to run errands, to hold a pine-knot at night lighting his father at a job, or to carry water, fill the woodbox, clean ashes from the fireplace, hoe weeds, pick berries, grapes, persimmons for beer-making. He hunted the timbers and came back with walnuts, hickory and hazel nuts… He went swimming with Austin Gollaher.

The Lincolns lived at Knob Creek from 1811 until 1816, and young Abe grew from a two-year-old toddler to a boy of seven. It was here that young Abraham nearly drowned in a rain-swollen creek and where his baby brother Thomas was born and died within days of his birth, to be buried in a neighbor's cemetery. And it was here, as at the Sinking Spring farm along Nolin Creek, that Thomas Lincoln once again ran into land problems with bad titles and faulty surveys. As with the farm on Nolin, Thomas would leave the Knob Creek farm under litigation and make his way to Indiana and the promise of secure land, thanks to Federal surveys.

The Knob Creek farm consisted of two hundred and twenty-eight acres, but it is not clear exactly how many acres Thomas actually owned. Like the Sinking Spring farm, its history traced back to a land grant in the 1790s. James Love took title to the farm tract in 1790 and sold it to George Lindsey in 1802. Lindsey, in

The McMurtry Map

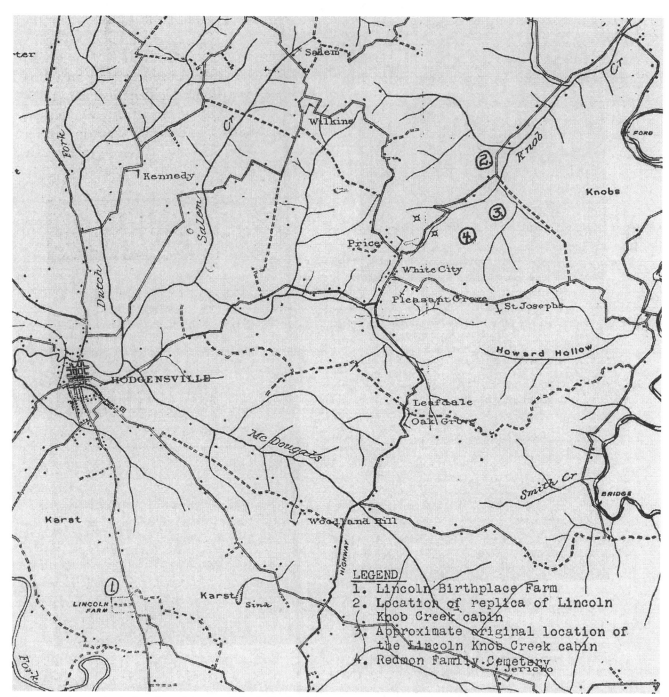

Long a mystery as to the location of the actual Knob Creek cabin, one can now place the cabin based on information gathered from several sources. R. Gerald McMurtry, an eminent historian and second director of the Lincoln National Library and Museum (Fort Wayne, Indiana), who grew up in the area and interviewed dozens of people associated with the Lincolns, concluded the Lincoln cabin was located atop Muldrough's Hill, adjoining the farm of George Redmon. According to neighbors who lived in the area, the Redmon farm was located approximately seventy-five yards from the family cemetery. The cemetery sits in an open field approximately one mile from the present-day Knob Creek cabin. When young Tommy Lincoln died, George Redmon offered space in his family cemetery atop the large Kentucky knob where the two families made their home.

From R. Gerald McMurtry, "Re-discovering the Supposed Grave of Lincoln's Brother," *Lincoln Herald*, vol. 48, no. 1 (February 1946), 16.

turn, sold the farm in 1811 to Lincoln, who would lose it in litigation over the faulty title.

The exact location of the Lincoln cabin, assumed by many to be the replica cabin located along the Bardstown road (Highway 31E), may never be known. Relying on statements by former neighbors of the two families that the Redmon cabin was seventy-five yards from the Redmon family cemetery, and that the Lincoln cabin adjoined the farm of George Redmon, Lincoln historian R. Gerald McMurtry placed the two cabins atop Muldrough's Hill a little over a mile from the current site of the replica cabin.

In January 1815, a Bill of Ejectment was brought against Thomas Lincoln and nine of his neighbors, involving various tracts of land within a ten-thousand-acre tract that had originally belonged to a man named Thomas Middleton, whose heirs lived in Philadelphia. Lincoln and George Lindsey were singled out as the first litigants as a test case. The case remained in the courts until 1818 when the jury brought in a verdict favoring Thomas Lincoln. Lincoln was awarded costs by the jury, but having settled in Indiana two years earlier, never collected his due. In 1820, a second judgment was rendered favoring, but again, he failed to collect his judgment. Title to the two hundred and twenty-eight acres had already reverted back to Lindsey who, following another round of litigation, saw the farm sold by a court commissioner. The site was privately owned and operated as both a tourist attraction and a working farm until 2001, when it became part of the National Park Service. The original "seven-acre field" continues to yield crops on an annual basis just as it did for Thomas Lincoln two hundred years ago.

Thomas Lincoln's tenure on the Knob Creek farm showed that he was prosperous among his neighbors. Court records list him as sixteenth among ninety-eight residents of the county in property value and show that only six other area residents owned more horses than he did. Records exist for at least two sales that Thomas Lincoln attended while at Knob Creek, which show that he purchased the highest priced heifer of three that were auctioned off for nine dollars and forty-two

and a half cents ($187 in 2015). At a second sale he purchased what appears to be a toy wagon for eight and a half cents ($1.79 in 2015), presumably for his young children.

Abraham Lincoln lived in the log cabin along the Knob Creek from when he was nearly three years old until he was well into his eighth year. It was the Knob Creek place where he had his earliest recollections. Here he recalled helping his father plant their "seven-acre field" only to awaken the next day and watch broken-hearted as the runoff from a big storm swept down the valley, carrying soil and seed with it. It was here in the rain-swollen Knob Creek that he fell one day while attempting to cross on a wet log. Unable to swim, he thrashed violently in the deep water, struggling to keep his head above water. His best friend, Austin Gollaher, rescued him by extending a broken tree limb to the foundering boy and pulling him to safety. And it was at Knob Creek on the fourth of July that he watched his father load his flintlock musket and, stepping outside the cabin, fire it into the air yelling "hurrah for the United States of America."

Turning seven, the young boy and his sister, two years older, walked the four mile round trip to "Blab" school; "blab" because lessons were read out loud. The school was a subscription school where students paid a fee to the teacher. It was run by Zachariah Riney and later by Caleb Hazel. It was under the stern teachings of Riney and Hazel that young Abraham learned to write. He was a quick learner and from his first efforts learned to write his name with glowing pride:

> Abraham Lincoln is my name
> And with my pen I wrote the same
> I wrote it both in haste and speed
> And left it here for fools to read

Now in the fall of 1816, beset by title troubles and litigation, Thomas Lincoln packed up his household goods and with Nancy, Sarah, and Abraham set out for Indiana where land titles and surveys were secure.

The family passed through Elizabethtown, Thomas and Nancy's first home together. They turned north and headed up the old Shepherdstown road toward the Mill Creek farm where "Granny" Bersheba Lincoln still kept house. They visited with the old lady and with Thomas's sister and brother-in-law before saying goodbye forever and heading west, making the sixty-mile trek across the Ohio River and into Spencer County, Indiana. Here Abraham would grow from a young boy to a grown man. He would soon learn the traits that would form the substance of his character. Here he would first experience overwhelming sorrow and sadness as he watched his mother die while still a young boy, and his beloved sister as a grown man.

Abraham Lincoln, sixteenth president of the United States, lived five years, 1811 to 1816, on this Knob Creek farm. Referring to his Kentucky years Abraham stated "My earliest recollection however, is of the Knob Creek place..." He and his sister, Sarah, attended their first school and their younger brother, Thomas Jr., was born and died here.

Early sign at the Knob Creek cabin site.
The site, originally privately owned, was
acquired by the National Park Service in 2001.

Knob Creek where a young Lincoln was saved from drowning by his boyhood friend Austin Gollaher.

Austin Gollaher 1806-1898

LINCOLN'S PLAYMATE

AUSTIN GOLLAHER
1806 — 1898
MARY HIS WIFE
1804 — 1873

I would rather see him than any man living.
Abraham Lincoln

Located in the present-day Pleasant Grove Baptist Church Cemetery near the Knob Creek farm of Thomas Lincoln is the grave of Austin Gollaher. Lincoln, while president, said, "I would rather see him than any man living." Lincoln and Gollaher were schoolmates and playmates at the time the family lived at Knob Creek. Gollaher later claimed to have saved the young Lincoln's life by pulling him from a swollen Knob Creek where Lincoln had fallen while attempting to cross the creek on a fallen log. The photograph of Gollaher is from a tintype ca. 1885. The tombstone is a modern replacement.

Austin Gollaher Home

The rear extension of the home is the original cabin of the Gollaher family at the time Abraham Lincoln lived at the Knob Creek farm. Lincoln visited this cabin on numerous occasions as a young boy. It is claimed that these logs were the ones used in the reconstruction of the cabin currently displayed at the Abraham Lincoln Boyhood Home at Knob Creek, making it the oldest surviving sentinel (1811-1816) to the life of Abraham Lincoln.

The Big Field

"The place on Knob Creek I remember very well. Our farm was composed of three fields. It lay in the valley surrounded by high hills and deep gorges. Sometimes when there came a big rain in the hills the water would come down through the gorges and spread all over the farm. The last thing that I remember doing there was one Saturday afternoon; the other boys planted the corn in what we called the big field – it contained seven acres – and I dropped the pumpkin seed. I dropped two seeds every other hill and every other row. The next Sunday morning there came a big rain in the hills; it did not rain a drop in the valley, but the water coming down through the gorges washed ground, corn, pumpkin seeds and all clear off the field." Abraham Lincoln

Muldrough's Hill. The Redmon and Lincoln cabins along with the Redmon cemetery are located just beyond the top of this knob.

The George Redmon Family Cemetery

The family cemetery of George Redmon, Thomas Lincoln's nearest neighbor. The cemetery contains twenty-one graves, seventeen arranged in two rows with four graves irregularly spaced. The cemetery, privately owned, was once marked by a dead walnut tree beside which a sunken grave containing a stone marker with the initials "T L" was discovered. The stone marker confirmed local tradition that the baby Lincoln was buried in the Redmon cemetery and that he was named Thomas.

The Grave of Tommy Lincoln

The George Redmon cemetery as it appeared in the 1950s, depicted on a postcard. The tall walnut tree (far left) bears a small sign attached by men of the Works Progress Administration identifying the grave of Tommy Lincoln. The large headstone to the far right marks the grave of George Redmon, close neighbor and friend of Thomas Lincoln and owner of the small pioneer cemetery. Redmon helped Thomas Lincoln bury the baby Lincoln believed to have died an infant in 1811.
From an early postcard.

The Redmon cemetery as it appeared in the early 1990s overgrown with grasses. The walnut tree stands as a sentinel marking the grave of Tommy Lincoln. It is this tree that led the author to the gravesite of Tommy Lincoln. The only stone visible above the tall grass is that of George Redmon.

This modern stone marking Tommy Lincoln's grave was placed by members of Post 15 (Des Moines, Iowa) of the Boy Scouts of America, in 1959.

Also a brother, younger than himself, who died in infancy.
Abraham Lincoln

Sometime shortly after moving into the cabin at Knob Creek, Nancy Lincoln gave birth to her third child, a son. Very little is known about the boy other than his name, Thomas, and the brief reference to him by Lincoln in his biographical sketch that he prepared for John Locke Scripps: "He [Abraham Lincoln] had a sister, older than himself, who was grown and married, but died many years ago, leaving no child, and also a brother, younger than himself, who died in infancy." The fact that the infant was named, coupled with Lincoln's statement that he died in infancy, supports the notion that the child did not die in childbirth, but survived for some period of time following his birth. More than this is not known.

What is known, after two hundred years, is that the child was buried in the cemetery of Thomas Lincoln's friend and neighbor, George Redmon. Early historians were not sure where the gravesite was located until 1933 when a group of Works Progress Administration (WPA) workers were clearing the Redmon family cemetery and recording the gravestones. The workmen uncovered seventeen marked graves arranged in two rows and a third row containing four irregularly spaced graves. Among the latter four was a partially sunken grave located next to a large walnut tree. Buried just below the surface the workmen found an angular-shaped stone bearing the initials "T L" inscribed "in a peculiar pioneer pattern." The engraved stone with its special letters revived an old neighborhood tradition among local families that Thomas Lincoln had buried his infant son in George Redmon's family cemetery.

To further support the claim, the initials carved into the stone marker bear a striking resemblance with another set of initials carved into the back panel of a corner cabinet made by Thomas Lincoln dated 1814, the same time period of young Tommy Lincoln's death. Historians have come to accept that the Redmon gravesite and engraved stone are those of Thomas Lincoln, Abraham Lincoln's younger brother.

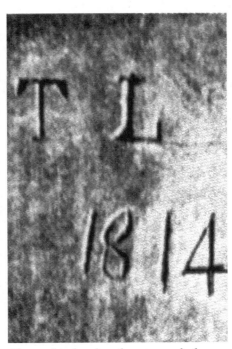

The homemade gravestone found by WPA workers in 1933 while clearing the cemetery. The stone was sunken beneath the earth atop the grave of Tommy Lincoln in the George Redmon cemetery. The stone is in the possession of Lincoln scholar Carl Howell of Hodgenville, Kentucky. Note the style of the two letters denoting Thomas Lincoln.
Photograph by Carl Howell.

The carving found on the rear panel of a corner cabinet made by Thomas Lincoln in 1814. The style of the carved letters match those on the tombstone marking Tommy Lincoln's grave. The cabinet is located in the Speed Art Museum in Louisville, Kentucky.
Photograph by R. Gerald McMurtry.

The grave of Tommy Lincoln discovered by WPA workers in 1933. A temporary wooden marker was placed on the gravesite following its discovery and excavation of the tombstone. To the left of the photograph is the large walnut tree that marks the location of the grave. Photograph by R. Gerald McMurtry.

The "ABC" School

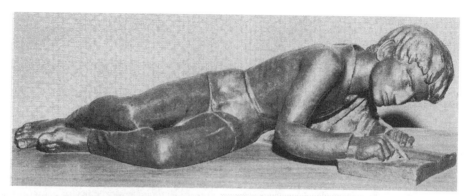

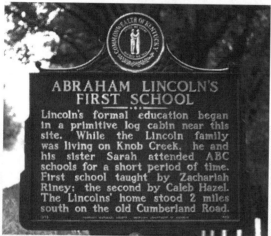

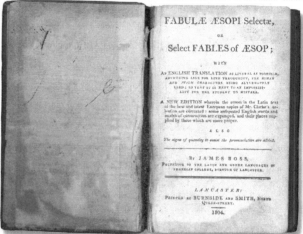

Top: "Lincoln at Seven," by sculptor Freeman Lorenz Schoolcraft. In 1947 the life-size bronze statue was presented to the Lincoln School in Dixon, Illinois (now closed). The statue's new home is in the Lincoln Library in the Jefferson School, Dixon, Illinois. Photo source: Mabel Kunkle, photo by A. R. Gustafson. *Left: Historical marker near the site of the "ABC" school attended by Lincoln and his sister, Sarah. Right: One of the earliest books young Abraham Lincoln read was Aesop's Fables. He later said that he had read it so many times he could rewrite the book from memory without the loss of a single word. Below: The "ABC" school cabin attended by Lincoln and Sarah. Referred to as a "Blab" school because the children read their lessons out loud. (This only known photograph of the school is superimposed on a typical rural background.)*

"If a stranger supposed to understand Latin, happened to sojourn in the neighborhood, he was looked upon as a wizard."
Abraham Lincoln

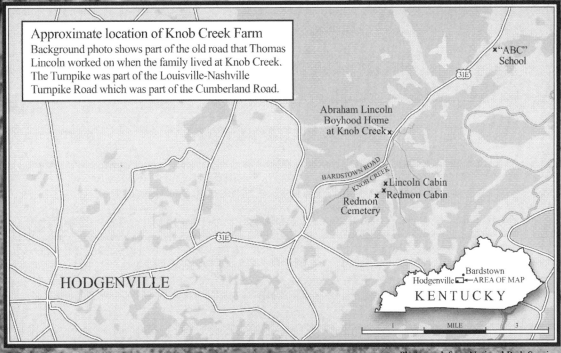

Approximate location of Knob Creek Farm
Background photo shows part of the old road that Thomas
Lincoln worked on when the family lived at Knob Creek.
The Turnpike was part of the Louisville-Nashville
Turnpike Road which was part of the Cumberland Road.

x "ABC"
School

31E

Abraham Lincoln
Boyhood Home
at Knob Creek x

BARDSTOWN ROAD

KNOB CREEK

x Lincoln Cabin
x Redmon Cabin
x
Redmon
Cemetery

31E

HODGENVILLE

Bardstown
Hodgenville □ ←AREA OF MAP

KENTUCKY

MILE

Photograph from National Park Service.

Nancy Hanks Lincoln

This portrait by Lincoln scholar and artist Lloyd Ostendorf portrays the young and beautiful mother of Abraham Lincoln. Developed from years of study of Lincoln's physical characteristics and contemporaries' descriptions of Nancy, the artist created his impression of what she might have looked like.

The light of Lincoln's young life and the source of early knowledge and education, Nancy used the family Bible as Lincoln's first primer. From her tender instruction he developed a deep knowledge of the testaments which he would use so effectively in later life. The harshness of the frontier must have been softened on many occasions by the young mother who Abraham and Sarah loved very much. Her death, when Lincoln was in his tenth year and Sarah in her twelfth, was devastating to them both. Lincoln learned to live with tragedy; this would be the first of four deaths of those closest to him and part of his own flesh. Perhaps from such sorrowful moments Lincoln learned a compassion that went far in guiding him through his momentous work as our greatest statesman.

Painting located in the Nancy Hanks Lincoln Hall, Lincoln Boyhood National Memorial, Indiana.

Nancy Hanks Lincoln

West Virginian
1784-1818

God bless my mother; all that I am or ever hope to be I owe to her. Abraham Lincoln

A few miles south of the town of Keyser, West Virginia, the highway splits abruptly with one fork turning east then south, making its way into a narrow valley that rests between two mountain ridges, and into the village of Antioch. Just south of Antioch a weather-beaten sign invites the driver to turn down a narrow, one-lane road to one of West Virginia's best kept secrets. The faded letters carved into the wooden sign read, "Birthplace of Nancy Hanks, mother of President Lincoln." Unknown to most followers of Abraham Lincoln, the site remains obscure and seldom visited. To the few who believe the site is the true birthplace of Lincoln's mother, it holds mystical significance.

In 1925, William E. Barton, a Congregational minister and Lincoln historian from Foxboro, Massachusetts, interested in Lincoln and his early years, published *The Lineage of Lincoln*, in which he examined the genealogy of both sides of Lincoln's family. The book focused heavily on the nativity and ancestry of Nancy Hanks, Lincoln's mother. Barton concluded that Lincoln's mother was not born in Tidewater, Virginia, as commonly believed, but was born in Hampshire County, Virginia (now Mineral County, West Virginia), along a small creek known as Mike's Run at the foot of New Creek Mountain. Barton, a meticulous researcher, based his conclusion on several primary records that he uncovered in various courthouses in Virginia, West Virginia, and Kentucky. Armed with his data and convinced of his findings, Barton took his case to the state of West Virginia. Governor William G. Connelly, acting on Barton's request, appointed a commission and charged it with the task of investigating "the authenticity of the location of the birthplace of Nancy Hanks on Mike's

Lincoln scholar William E. Barton (left foreground) stands on what he believed to be the site of Joseph Hanks's cabin at the foot of New Creek Mountain in Hampshire County, West Virginia. Photograph taken in 1929. Courtesy of *Piedmont Herald*, Piedmont, West Virginia.

Run." On September 21, 1929, the commission met in the town of Moorefield and decided unanimously to accept Barton's conclusion.

One day later, on Sunday, September 22, a ceremony was held at the site identified by Barton as the original cabin location of the pioneer Joseph Hanks, believed to be the grandfather of Nancy Hanks. Barton told the small gathering, "Here, just at the close of the struggle that gave to the American colonies their independence was born a little girl for whom was reserved the illustrious maternity of Abraham Lincoln."

By 1933, the state had acquired part of the original farm and erected a replica cabin and stone memorial identifying the site as the birthplace of Nancy Hanks. By 1966, however, the official position taken by the state of West Virginia in 1929 had softened somewhat. In that year, Governor Hulett C. Smith, in a letter to a real estate developer who was seeking historic status for the farm site, wrote: "At this time there exists among historians some serious doubt as to whether the location is the birthplace of Nancy Hanks, and it is my belief that we should have the results of some concrete historical research before a final decision is made on this."

Governor Smith sought the advice of several authoritative sources on the question of Nancy Hanks's birthplace. The West Virginia Division of Parks and Recreation, the West Virginia Department of Archives and History, the Travel Development Division, the Antiquity Division, and the Library of Congress each responded to the question of where Nancy Hanks was born. Their responses failed to resolve the question: "Your observation that there is considerable controversy over the correct birthplace of Abraham Lincoln's mother is accurate. Historians have not been able to determine with any certainty where she was born." The question, however, is which historians were they referring to and had they examined Barton's research with care? Carl Sandburg was one of the historians who led the assault on Barton's claim. Had they carefully examined Barton's research and not Sandburg's, they would have had no doubt that Nancy Hanks was born in what is now West Virginia.

To answer the question of where Nancy Hanks was born one must first know when she was born. Once we know the year of her birth we need only determine where her mother, Lucy Hanks, was on that date. Where Lucy was, so was Nancy.

Primary documents pertaining to Nancy Hanks are scarce, but there is one document that bears directly on her birth: it is the Lincoln family Bible. Carl Sandburg, in his book on Oliver R. Barrett's collection of Lincolniana, *Lincoln Collector*, writes of the genealogical data that Lincoln himself wrote in the Lincoln-Johnston family Bible. According to Sandburg, shortly after Lincoln's father died in 1851, Lincoln visited his parents' home in Coles County, Illinois, and made entries into the family Bible, listing birth, death, and marriage information about the two families. At some time following Lincoln's death, Dennis Hanks removed the page from the Bible and kept it, presumably as a souvenir. Jesse Weik, who collaborated on a biography of Lincoln with William Herndon, located the missing page in the possession of a daughter of Dennis Hanks. Dennis "tore out and wrote out the Bible record." When the page was finally recovered it was worn and tattered with a small portion missing from its upper corner. The missing portion is alleged to contain the birth and marriage dates of Lincoln's parents written in Lincoln's hand. All was not lost, however, as John D. Johnston, Lincoln's stepbrother, copied the entire page from the family Bible into a ledger book before Dennis removed it. John J. Hall, a grandson of Lincoln's stepmother and a second cousin to Lincoln, who lived with Lincoln's parents in the family cabin at Goosenest Prairie, also copied the record from the Bible before Dennis Hanks removed it.

The missing piece of the page recorded separately by both Johnston and Hall reads, "Thomas Lincoln was born Jan 6, 1778, and was married June 12, 1806, to Nancy Hanks, who was born Feb 5, 1784." The Johnston and Hall copies are the best evidence for Nancy Hanks's birthdate being February 5, 1784.

This brings us to the question where was Nancy Hanks born? Wherever Nancy's mother lived in February 1784, you can be sure was the birthplace of Nancy Hanks.

Most historians accept the theory that Nancy Hanks was the illegitimate daughter of Lucy Hanks, and that Lucy was one of four sisters whose father was a man named Joseph Hanks who died in Nelson County, Kentucky, in 1793. This theory can be traced to three individuals, all closely associated with Lincoln: William H. Herndon, Dennis Hanks, and John Hanks. Dennis and John were nephews of Lucy Hanks and the grandsons of Joseph Hanks.

*View of the reconstructed cabin of Joseph Hanks
in Hampshire County, West Virginia.*

The basis for believing Nancy Hanks was illegitimate is attributable to William Herndon, Lincoln's long-standing law partner, while Lucy being the daughter of Joseph Hanks is attributable to Dennis and John Hanks.

Barton accepted the statements of Dennis and John Hanks that Lucy Hanks was one of four daughters of Joseph Hanks. It formed the basis of his claim that Nancy Hanks was born in Hampshire County, (West) Virginia. Barton concentrated his efforts on a search of courthouse records in an attempt to track Joseph Hanks's whereabouts during the critical period of Nancy Hanks's birth. His research took him to the Tidewater region of Virginia where he uncovered numerous documents listing members of the Hanks family. In Richmond County, Virginia, Barton found references to a Joseph Hanks he believed was later the Joseph Hanks of Nelson County, Kentucky.

Barton was able to reconstruct Joseph's whereabouts beginning with his birth in 1725 and continuing through 1782, after which Joseph no longer appears in the Richmond County records. On February 28, 1787, five years after the last record in Richmond County, Joseph purchased a farm on the Rolling Fork of the Salt River in Nelson County, Kentucky.

Barton had pieced together a documentary trail that took Joseph Hanks from Richmond County, Virgina, to Nelson County, Kentucky, with a gap of five years in between. He set out to fill the gap between the two periods, trying to locate Joseph in the intervening years of 1782 to 1787. He began by searching the United States Census records making up a who's who of Hankses during this period. He found a single listing for a Joseph Hanks with a family of eleven individuals living in Hampshire County, (West) Virginia, for the year 1782. Barton found no other listing for a Joseph Hanks in any of the records he searched covering the period. He wrote, "This [eleven white persons] was a family of precisely what it should have been to include Joseph Hanks, his wife, five sons and four daughters, including Lucy."

Barton supported his Hampshire County claim as the interim home of Joseph and his family by discovering a document in the military pension archives for Thomas Hanks, born 1759, who was drafted into militia service while living in Hampshire County. He was drafted in the fall of 1780 for a period of three months. After returning home to Hampshire County, he served again for two months in the winter of 1781. Although ineligible for a pension, having failed to serve the minimum six months, Thomas still went ahead and filed a claim, leaving a record of his service. Barton wrote, "Beyond any doubt this Thomas Hanks is Joseph's son." Both the date of his birth and his residence in Hampshire County fit Barton's thesis. Joseph's will named a son, Thomas, born in 1759, which made a perfect fit. According to Barton, Thomas preceded his father to Hampshire County in 1780. Barton believes he then sent word back to his father to come to Hampshire County and bring the rest of the family.

Barton's final and best piece of evidence involved Joseph Hanks's Hampshire County property. On March 9, 1784, Joseph took out a small mortgage on his interest in a 108-acre farm along Mike's Run. Six months later, in

View of Doll's Gap located on Saddle Mountain. The view is looking east toward New Creek Mountain. Doll's Gap served as a natural passageway through the mountain range for settlers moving west. The symmetrical shape of the gap led to naming the ridge "Saddle Mountain."

*Bronze plaque located on stone stele
at cabin site. The plaque reads:*

THIS TABLET MARKS THE SITE
OF THE CABIN WHERE
NANCY HANKS
LINCOLN'S MOTHER
WAS BORN
1782 [sic]
ERECTED BY
NANCY HANKS ASSOCIATION
1933

September 1784, the mortgage was foreclosed and all traces of Joseph and his family of eleven disappeared from Hampshire County; presumably they migrated to Kentucky where they appear two and a half years later in 1787.

Barton had uncovered a series of documents that formed a continuous timeline from 1725 to 1793, running through three counties and ending in Kentucky. Although the records were sparse, they fit neatly together. Barton supported his claim that Joseph lived in Hampshire County before moving to Kentucky by claiming that the Hampshire County Joseph was the only Joseph Hanks found in any of the records for that period, and that Thomas Hanks of Hampshire County was a perfect fit for Joseph's oldest son.

If Barton is correct, and there is no reason to question his research, Lucy Hanks gave birth to her daughter Nancy while living with her father Joseph in Hampshire County, Virginia. As the daughter of Joseph Hanks, Lucy would be expected to be under his and his wife's care at the time of Nancy's birth.

The replica cabin situated along Mike's Run in what is now Mineral County, West Virginia, deserves recognition as one of the important memorial sites closely associated with Abraham Lincoln.

Mike's Run at the foot of New Creek Mountain. The reconstructed cabin is located a few hundred feet from this clear-running brook.

> *She* [Lincoln's mother] *was the illegitimate daughter of Lucy Hanks and a well-bred Virginia farmer or planter.*
>
> William Henry Herndon

My mother was a bastard, was the daughter of a nobleman, so called, of Virginia... My mother inherited his qualities and I hers. All that I am or hope ever to be I get from my mother, God bless her.
Abraham Lincoln to William H. Herndon

Nancy Lincoln's heritage is indeed obscure. She may have been illegitimate, or at least Lincoln may have believed that she was.
Don E. Fehrenbacher

[Lincoln] *said, among other things, that she* [Nancy Hanks Lincoln] *was the illegitimate daughter of Lucy Hanks and a well-bred Virginia farmer or planter; and he argued that from this last source came his power of analysis, his logic, his mental activity, his ambition, and all the qualities that distinguish him from the other members and descendants of the Hanks family.*
William Henry Herndon

Was she, or wasn't she?

Of all the mothers of all the presidents, none is more shrouded in mystery or bounded by controversy than Nancy Hanks Lincoln. Among the more learned students of Lincoln's ancestry, there is little agreement on the details of her birth and early life. Professional historians have shied away from any serious study of her nativity, leaving the controversy to the non-professionals to fight over.

Depending on which biographer is read, Nancy Hanks was born in as many as three different places to as many as four different sets of parents. Her birth date is variously listed as 1783, 1784, and 1785. At one time considered a common-law wife, she was eventually rescued from that ignominy by the discovery of legal documents legitimizing her marriage. Even so, Nancy Hanks Lincoln still wanders through dozens of histories in search of legitimacy.

Abraham Lincoln himself, it seems, believed that his mother was born out of wedlock. But, he took solace in the belief that his maternal grandfather was "a well-bred Virginia farmer or planter," and it was from him that he believed he inherited "his power of analysis, his logic, his mental activity, and his ambition."

Today there are two schools of thought on the question of Nancy's birth. The first believes her born out of wedlock, the father a Virginia planter as Lincoln is allegedly said to have believed, while the second defends her legitimate birth, her father being James Hanks, the son of Joseph Hanks. James died shortly after Nancy's birth, leaving her mother Lucy a widow. Despite the passage of over one hundred and fifty years since William Herndon's original research on Abraham Lincoln's life, and despite the fact that most academic historians discredit many aspects of Herndon's biographical study, he still remains the source for those who believe Nancy was born out of wedlock. Opposing Herndon are those who subscribe to the early studies of one of the more highly respected Lincoln scholars, Louis A. Warren. Today, the debate has cooled considerably, for the majority of historians and most biographers simply slide past the question, relegating it to a minor or inconsequential aspect of Lincoln's life.

William H. Herndon
Library of Congress

The case of Nancy Hanks Lincoln illustrates just how subjective many aspects of written history have often become where yards of whole cloth are often woven from small skeins of thread. While much of what we know of Lincoln's birth is based on hearsay, there is one thing we can be sure of concerning his origin:

Nancy Hanks Lincoln is the president's mother. Beyond that single fact no documentation exists establishing absolute proof of Nancy Hanks Lincoln's own ancestry or birth status, including the name of her own mother and father. All discussion concerning Nancy Hanks's circumstances relative to her birth and her ancestry are circumstantial. No documentary records, other than Lincoln's notations in a family Bible in his own hand, are known to exist establishing her birth date or her biological parents. And herein lies the problem.

While the historical community accepts Nancy Hanks's illegitimate birth based solely on Herndon's statement, the best argument for her legitimacy is that made by Louis A. Warren who concluded that Nancy Hanks's mother was not a Hanks at all, but a Shipley (Lucy Shipley) who married a Hanks (James Hanks), gave birth to a daughter (Nancy Hanks) and was widowed shortly thereafter. Thus young Lucy Hanks was married for a brief period before giving birth to her daughter, Nancy. Warren believes that in 1790, Nancy's mother, the widowed Lucy Shipley Hanks, married Henry Sparrow and bore nine children by him. Following Lucy's marriage to Henry Sparrow, young Nancy was sent to the household of Lucy's older sister Rachel Shipley Berry and her husband Richard Berry, Sr., who raised her as one of their own. This part of the story is fact. Among the few documents associated with Lucy Hanks and her daughter Nancy is a marriage bond between Thomas Lincoln and Nancy Hanks bearing the signature of Richard Berry, Jr., as Nancy's then legal guardian. This important fact has been passed over in much of the literature save for the writing of Louis A. Warren.

The death of Thomas Lincoln's father in 1786, at the hands of an Indian marauding party, left Thomas's mother, Bersheba, a widow with five young children. She left their home on Long Run near Louisville, Kentucky, and moved the family to the Beech Fork community several miles to the southeast. Living close by was the family of Richard Berry, Sr., and his young ward, Nancy Hanks. It was here that Thomas and Nancy first became acquainted and eventually fell in love. And it was here that Thomas Lincoln and Nancy Hanks were married in 1806.

Much of the study surrounding Nancy Hanks genealogy is confounded by the relative paucity

The Lincoln Kinsman was a monthly publication produced by Louis A. Warren devoted to the kith and kin of Abraham Lincoln. Warren concentrated his research on the genealogy of the Lincolns and Hankses.

of documents in the files of the numerous pioneer courthouses as to where she and her ancestors lived, and by the finding that during the period covered by her short life there were over a dozen different Nancy Hankses that appear in the few records that do exist. In addition, Nancy and her relations moved about during her early life, living in as many as three states: Virginia, North Carolina, and Kentucky. While the large number of Nancy Hankses and their precise locale at any given date has confused some researchers, it is the paucity of documents that has limited most, forcing them to accept tradition that bears a certain subjectivity in its conclusions.

The earliest tradition that supports Nancy's illegitimate birth is that told by William H. Herndon and eventually published by him. Herndon's principal source for Lincoln's nativity was Lincoln himself. In his book, *Life of Lincoln*, Herndon wrote, "He [Lincoln] said, among other things, that she [his mother] was the illegitimate daughter of Lucy Hanks and a well-bred Virginia farmer or planter." This statement is, of course, hearsay and must be taken as fact without proof if we are to accept the illegitimate birth of Nancy Hanks.

However, if Lincoln did believe his mother to be illegitimate, he must have learned the fact from some other person, presumably later in life. It is not likely that Nancy would have told her nine-year-old son she was illegitimate. Equally improbable is the idea that Lincoln's father would have told him his mother was illegitimate. Who then, told Lincoln about his mother's illegitimate birth? The likely candidate for such a revelation would be Dennis Hanks. Where Dennis learned of Nancy's illegitimate birth, if true, is unknown. He was born fifteen years after Nancy's birth and nine years after his Aunt Lucy Hanks married Henry Sparrow. He did not live with his biological mother, also named Nancy Hanks, but was raised by Elizabeth, Lucy's sister (or sister-in-law), and Thomas Sparrow, who might have known the details if such were true.

In a letter to Herndon, Dennis made a statement that has carried the day for later historians. In the letter dated April 2, 1866, Dennis wrote, "My Mother and Abe's Mothers Mother war Sisters My Mothers Name was Nancy Hanks Abes Grand Mother was Lucy Hanks which was my Mothers Sister the woman that Raised me was Elizabeth Sparrow the Sister of Lucy and Nancy The other Sister hir name was polly Friend so you See that there was four Sisters that was Hankses."

Those historians who come down on the side of Nancy's illegitimacy accept Dennis Hanks's statement verbatim and claim that a man by the name of Joseph Hanks, progenitor of the Kentucky Hanks family, was the

Dennis Hanks
From a carte de visite

father of Lucy Hanks and therefore, the grandfather of Nancy Hanks. Joseph Hanks left a will that lists eight children. Among the eight children are three girls, sisters, mentioned by Dennis Hanks: Elizabeth, Nancy, and Polly. Significantly, Joseph Hanks does not list Lucy as one of his children in his will. Supporters of the illegitimacy side dismiss this omission by concluding that the absence of Lucy from the will is a result of her being disowned (for adultery), or simply because she received her inheritance from Joseph while still alive, negating her claim after he died. These conclusions are confounded, however, by Joseph specifying in his will that his property was to be distributed to "all my children." The omission of Lucy from "all my children" is a serious omission, and not so lightly dismissed. If not Joseph Hanks's daughter, whose daughter was Lucy?

Louis A. Warren claims Lucy Hanks was not the daughter of Joseph Hanks (or the sister of Nancy Hanks, Dennis's mother), but rather the daughter-in-law. Traditional (oral) evidence from several individuals states that Lucy married a man named James Hanks, believed to be a son of Joseph Hanks, deceased at the time Joseph wrote his will, who fathered Nancy and died soon thereafter. This tradition also states that Lucy was a Shipley, not a Hanks, and one of three Shipley sisters. Proponents of this theory conclude that Dennis Hanks was mistaken about "four sisters," there being three sisters and a sister-in-law. If true, none of the relationships as far as Dennis Hanks and Lucy and Nancy Hanks would change. Aunts would still be aunts and cousins would still be cousins. This is an important point when sifting through family history.

Additional support comes from two documents, which exist relative to Lucy and her daughter Nancy. Kentucky law in 1806 required a bond be given before issuing a marriage license. The bridegroom and the bride's father usually signed such bonds. In Nancy's case, being without a father, Richard Berry, Jr., signed the bond as her guardian. This supports the theory that Nancy's father was dead and her next of kin under Kentucky law was Richard Berry, Jr., who now acted as her guardian. This Richard Berry is the same Richard Berry, Jr., in whose house in the Beech Fork community Nancy was living at the time, and in whose cabin she married Thomas Lincoln in 1806. His father was Richard Berry, Sr., whose wife was Rachel Shipley. Proponents of the legitimacy theory claim Lucy was Rachel's sister. When Lucy married Henry Sparrow, her six-year-old daughter Nancy was sent to live with her Aunt Rachel and Uncle Richard, Sr. Nancy eventually moved into the home of their son, Richard Berry, Jr., who then became Nancy's legal guardian and, as such, signed her marriage bond.

Prior to her marriage to Henry Sparrow in 1790, Lucy Hanks was required to give her affirmation as to her age and willingness for a marriage license to be issued. This

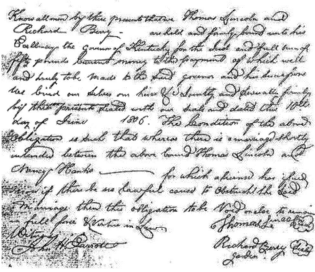

The marriage bond of Thomas Lincoln pledging his intent to marry Nancy Hanks. Richard Berry, Jr., signed the agreement as Nancy Hanks's guardian, suggesting he was her closest next of kin. Kentucky law required a woman's father sign the marriage bond and, if deceased, the closest male sign in the father's stead.

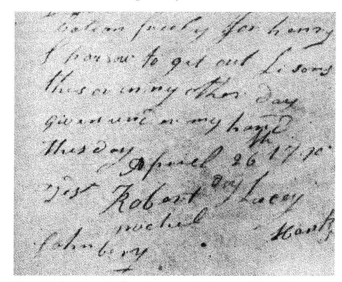

Lucy Hanks's signed affirmation agreeing to marry Henry Sparrow in which she signs her name with the addition of the word "doy" that Louis A. Warren believes was originally "widoy."

affirmation was signed by Lucy Hanks and attested to by John Berry who was a brother of Richard Berry, Jr. This document bears the signature of "Lucey Hanks" with the word "doy" preceding her signature. Louis A. Warren maintains this is part of the word "widoy" supporting his contention that Lucy Hanks was previously married. The word "doy" may be a partial spelling with the "wi" badly faded. Without further forensic examination it is impossible to tell.

The truth of Nancy Lincoln's birth may never be resolved. The two schools of thought on the subject rely exclusively on traditional accounts and cannot be proven by a single piece of documentary evidence. The oral traditions are, of course, contradictory, and the few documents that do exist are purely circumstantial. Joseph Hanks's will is negative on the subject, and can only be explained by presumptive arguments as to why Lucy Hanks is omitted. The Lucy Hanks affirmation note and the Nancy Hanks marriage bond attested to by the Berry brothers, while suggestive, is also inconclusive. Oral traditions are helpful in many ways, but cannot be used as proof. The literature is replete with cases involving Abraham Lincoln where prominent individuals have given sworn testimony to incidents and events that never occurred.

The assumption that Lucy Hanks was one of four daughters of Joseph Hanks by Dennis Hanks (a grandson) is understandable. Dennis was born nearly ten years after Lucy and Henry Sparrow married. It is not unreasonable to believe that Dennis Hanks understood the four aunts to be sisters rather than three sisters and a sister-in-law. The Hanks, Berry, and Shipley families all lived within the same region of Amelia County, Virginia, and several members migrated together to Nelson County, Kentucky. Nancy Hanks lived for a while in the home of Richard Berry, Sr., and was married in the cabin home of Richard Berry, Jr., her guardian according to her marriage bond.

The oral tradition supporting Herndon's conclusion that Lucy Hanks was the daughter of Joseph Hanks who gave birth to a daughter out of wedlock falls considerably short of proven when considered alongside the oral tradition and documentary material claiming Lucy a Shipley and daughter-in-law to Joseph Hanks. The documents which do exist show no Hanks as guardian or next of kin to either Lucy Hanks or Nancy Hanks, supporting the contention that Lucy's maiden name was not Hanks, and that Nancy was the product of Lucy's marriage to a Hanks, a Hanks that died leaving Nancy's legal guardianship under the laws of Kentucky to her male next of kin, a Berry.

Lincoln's birth in a simple log cabin to an illegitimate mother is often cited in an effort to contrast his lowly beginning with his rise to greatness. In doing so, Lincoln has become the archetypal representative of the American dream. The fact is, however, whether Lincoln rose from a mudsill beginning or was born of an illegitimate mother, his stature as America's greatest president is secure.

She was.

Science has recently entered the debate presumably solving the question by analyzing the mitochondrial DNA from matrilineal descendants of both the Hanks and Shipley families. Mitochondrial DNA is inherited solely through the maternal line. By comparing certain regions within the mitochondrial DNA, biologists can determine the relationship between individuals. Because mitochondrial DNA is transmitted only through the maternal line and has a very low mutation rate, it is a powerful tool in determining relationships among female individuals.

While there are no descendants of Nancy Hanks Lincoln, there are living descendants of Ann Lee Hanks, (Nancy Hanks's grandmother in the accepted lineage), descendants of two daughters of Lucy Hanks from her marriage to Henry Sparrow, and of Rachel Shipley and Naomi Shipley (sisters of Lucy Hanks in the Warren scenario). Family Tree DNA, a commercial company that provides DNA testing to the public, undertook the testing of seven of the descendants of the Hanks and Shipley families. The results concluded that Lucy Hanks was not a sister of Rachel and Naomi Shipley, but that she was a daughter of Ann Lee Hanks. These studies, if proven accurate, support the oral tradition espoused by Herndon, and later by William Barton, that Lucy Hanks was the daughter of Joseph Hanks who gave birth to a daughter out of wedlock, Nancy Hanks.

Partial Hanks Matrilineal Chart

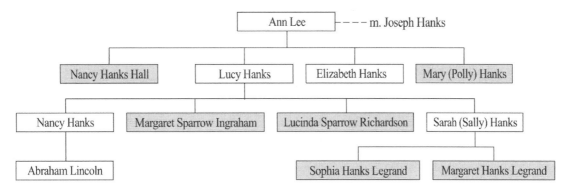

Mitochondrial DNA (mtDNA) was analyzed from contemporary descendants of the individuals shown in shaded boxes, leading to the conclusion that Lucy Hanks was the daughter of Ann Lee Hanks and not related to the Shipley family.

Dennis Hanks, 1799-1892

From a carte de visite.

Dennis Hanks is the single most important informant on the early life of Abraham Lincoln and his Kentucky relations. Born in 1799, Dennis was ten years older than Lincoln. His mother, also named Nancy Hanks, was one of four daughters of Joseph Hanks, the father of Lucy Hanks.

Dennis was born out of wedlock and was taken into the family of Elizabeth Hanks Sparrow and her husband, Thomas Sparrow. Elizabeth was the sister of Nancy Hanks, Dennis's mother, and it was Thomas Sparrow's brother Henry who married Lucy Hanks in 1790.

In 1803, when Dennis was four years old, his foster parents, Elizabeth and Thomas Sparrow, moved into the home of Lucy and Henry Sparrow in Mercer County, Kentucky, where they stayed for three years before returning to their home in Hardin County. Dennis lived in the home of Elizabeth and Thomas Sparrow from the age of four until the age of nineteen. Elizabeth and Thomas, although acting as foster parents to Dennis, were in fact his aunt and uncle. At the time Abraham Lincoln was born in 1809, Dennis, age ten, lived within three miles of the birthplace cabin. When Thomas Lincoln moved his family to Indiana in 1816, Thomas, Elizabeth, and young Dennis, now seventeen, followed.

When the epidemic of the "milk sickness" hit the small community near Little Pigeon Creek in 1818, both Thomas and Elizabeth Sparrow died, followed a few days later by Nancy Lincoln. Now alone and "orphaned," Dennis, nineteen years old, moved into the small cabin of widower Thomas Lincoln, becoming a close member of the Lincoln family.

In 1819, Thomas Lincoln returned to Elizabethtown where he married Sarah Bush Johnston. Sarah, a widow with three children of her own, moved with her children to the Lincoln cabin in Indiana.

In 1821 Dennis married Elizabeth Johnston, a daughter of Sarah Bush Johnston Lincoln and stepsister of Abraham Lincoln, bringing him even closer into the Lincoln family circle. When Thomas Lincoln moved his family to Illinois in 1830, Dennis and his family went with them. Dennis Hanks lived to be 92 years old and died when run over by a carriage while returning from a special emancipation celebration.

At the time of Lincoln's death in 1865, Dennis was sixty-six years old. He had lived an obscure, frontier life, much of it "hardscrabble." Now, in his later years, he was suddenly thrust into star status. Within six weeks of Lincoln's death, Dennis had given his first interviews to William Herndon (June 6 and 13, 1865) in Chicago.

Clearly Dennis Hanks was a close, personal member of the Thomas Lincoln family and had much to offer about the Lincolns and his famous cousin Abraham. Just how reliable all of his reminiscences were is difficult to determine. In answering fourteen questions posed by William Herndon about the early Kentucky Lincolns, Dennis gave incorrect answers to all fourteen. Still, he proved to be a valuable source in describing life in those early days on the frontier.

John Hanks
From a carte de visite

Partial Genealogy of the Hanks Family
after William E. Barton

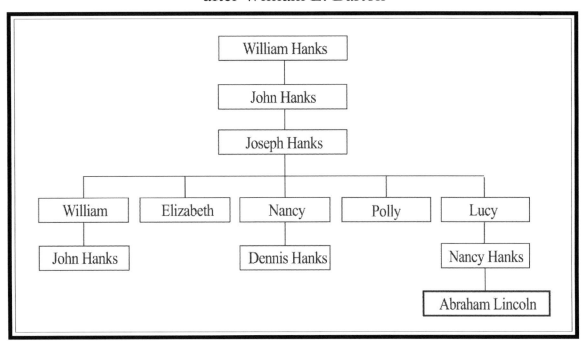

The genealogical tree depicted here is accepted by most historians. It shows the relationship of John Hanks and Dennis Hanks to Abraham Lincoln (cousins once removed). Dennis Hanks was the illegitimate son of Nancy Hanks, Abraham Lincoln's aunt. Dennis Hanks's mother Nancy has often been confused with Abraham Lincoln's mother Nancy in the literature, showing that great care must be taken when interpreting historical records and personal recollections.

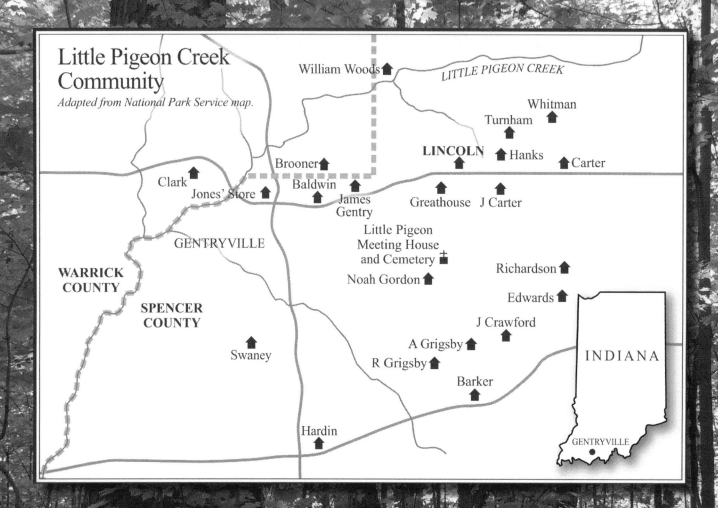

Little Pigeon Creek Community

Adapted from National Park Service map.

William Woods

LITTLE PIGEON CREEK

Whitman

Turnham

LINCOLN

Hanks

Carter

Brooner

Clark

Jones' Store

Baldwin

James Gentry

Greathouse

J Carter

Little Pigeon Meeting House and Cemetery

Richardson

GENTRYVILLE

Noah Gordon

Edwards

WARRICK COUNTY

SPENCER COUNTY

J Crawford

A Grigsby

R Grigsby

Swaney

Barker

INDIANA

Hardin

GENTRYVILLE

Indiana 1816-1830

The Formative Years

He [Thomas Lincoln] *removed from Kentucky to what is now Spencer County, Indiana, in my eighth year… It was a wild region, with many bears and other wild animals, still in the woods. There I grew up.* Abraham Lincoln

Thomas Lincoln's trouble with land titles continued to plague him throughout his years in Kentucky. Overlapping land grants traced back to colonial days led to a system of erroneous and confusing records of title. Faulty surveys only compounded the problem. It was not uncommon to find cases where the owners of certain parcels of land purchased the land two, three, or four times before they held clear title. Thus, the writings of early authors who claimed that Thomas Lincoln was unable to hold his land and prosper because of his shiftless or indolent nature are without foundation.

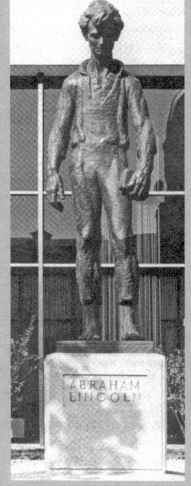

Thomas Lincoln's grief over ownership of his land was shared by virtually all his neighbors and a good part of the population of frontier Kentucky. The fault lay not in Thomas Lincoln's character, but in the state of the land records in Virginia, of which Kentucky was the western-most county during the country's earliest years.

At the time Thomas Lincoln sold the Mill Creek farm he lost thirty-eight acres, amounting to eighteen pounds sterling or almost twenty percent of his original investment. At Sinking Spring he lost most of his investment through a faulty title, including his down payment and court costs, and again at the Knob Creek place he, along with nine of his neighbors, was subject to an ejectment suit involving a ten-thousand-acre tract of land

Young Abe Lincoln, by David K. Rubins. The statue now stands in front of the Indiana Government Center South near the State House in Indianapolis.

The Old Cumberland Road was the main thoroughfare from Louisville in Kentucky to Nashville, Tennessee. When the Lincoln family began its migration to Indiana it followed this road as far as Elizabethtown. Photograph from R. Gerald McMurtry, *"The Lincoln Migration from Kentucky to Indiana,"* Indiana Magazine of History, vol. 33, no. 4 (December 1937).

Recreated "trace" by the National Park Service of the final leg of the journey in Indiana to the Lincolns' new farm. The overall journey covered approximately 100 miles and took two weeks to complete. The final few miles required cutting a new road through the wilderness to the new farm site.

held by the heirs of a Philadelphia merchant. These families were, for the most part, hard working, law abiding, church going, successful farmers who fell victim to land agents, land lawyers, and land mismanagement.

Now, in early December 1816, Thomas Lincoln had had enough of bad land management. He was pulling up stakes and moving his family to Indiana where the land was federally owned, the surveys were accurate, and the titles sure. Unlike in Kentucky, the titles were backed by the full guarantee of the United States government. For the first time in his thirty-eight years, Thomas Lincoln could purchase land without fear of ejectment, and all his hard labor would go directly to himself and his family rather than absentee owners and land attorneys.

At the time of his migration from the Knob Creek place to Indiana, Thomas Lincoln owned four horses, a wagon, and several items of household goods, including several pieces of furniture that he had made over the years since his marriage to Nancy. Also included in the family inventory were three books: the family Bible, Dilworth's Speller and *Aesop's Fables.* The latter of these three books is believed to have been a gift from Nancy Lincoln to her young son. The family Bible was carried by the Lincolns through all their travels and is the only item positively known to have been owned by the young family that remained with them throughout their lifetime and still survives today. It proved to be Lincoln's primer simply because it was the only book constantly present in the Lincoln household.

Thomas Lincoln made a preliminary trip into Indiana in the fall of 1816 during which time he selected a tract of land located in Perry County near the Little Pigeon Creek. The new site was only one hundred miles from the Knob Creek farm. The route travelled by the Lincoln family to Indiana is supported only by oral tradition and known facts about the people and places in the surrounding area at the time of the migration. While certain parts of the migration route are supported by consistent tradition from multiple sources, other parts are conflicting. By carefully researching the routes available in 1816 and the affidavits given by all parties living along the trail, Lincoln historian R. Gerald McMurtry summarized his findings as to the route with fair certainty. The initial phase of the journey followed the old Shepherdstown road north, remnants of which still pass through the Fort Knox military reservation.

The entire trip covered approximately one hundred miles and required the family to cross the Ohio River, which formed the boundary between Kentucky and Indiana. The trip took from twelve to fourteen days as a result of their stopping along the way to visit with family and friends. The principal stop was at the farm of Thomas Lincoln's sister and brother-in-law, Nancy and William Brumfield. Here the Lincoln family visited with Bersheba, Thomas's mother, and with the Brumfields and their four young daughters. The stay probably lasted two days, during which Abraham and his grandmother Bersheba saw each other for the first and last time. Here also, young Abraham and Sarah played with their cousins, who were similar ages.

After saying their farewells to Bersheba and the Brumfields, Thomas took his family west, then north to the Ohio River, crossing at Thompson's Ferry, which was located opposite the mouth of Anderson Creek on the Indiana side of the river. It was at Anderson Creek that a grown Abraham Lincoln would later operate his own ferry and face his first encounter with the law for ferrying the river without a duly authorized license. When Thomas Lincoln arrived at the ferry he joined some twelve to fifteen families already waiting to cross the river to Indiana. The caravan of emigrants totalled sixty-one people and took two days to ferry all of them across. The autumn rains had raised the river, requiring special care in transporting the long caravan of human cargo.

Thompson's Ferry was a substantial operation complying with all state regulations concerning ferries. These regulations required the ferryboat to be able to carry a large wagon and four horses per trip and to have a minimum of two able-bodied men on board at all times. Since the Lincoln entourage consisted of a wagon, four horses, and livestock, it is certain that it took at least two trips to ferry across all their possessions, living and otherwise.

The new homesite was located approximately sixteen miles to the northwest of where the Anderson Creek emptied into the Ohio River. Along the way the migrants passed the farm of Austin Lincoln, eldest son of Hananiah Lincoln, who had a farm twelve miles south of Thomas Lincoln's new home. Several miles to the northeast of the new home was the farm of Thomas's older brother, Josiah Lincoln. Both Austin and Josiah had moved from Kentucky to Indiana a few years earlier to escape the bad land records of Kentucky. Within four days' travel, Indiana was home to three Lincoln families, all refugees of Kentucky.

Once in Indiana, the party had to cut its way through the dense forest "with an ax felling the trees as they went." One observer noted that "the lowlands were so thick with underbrush that one could scarcely get through." Several of the early biographers of Abraham Lincoln described the early Indiana home of the Lincoln family as being a "half-faced camp" or three-sided shelter, which housed the new settlers for as much as a year. This primitive shelter became a feature of many children's books about Lincoln's early life, contrasting the hardships of frontier life with Lincoln's later success as president.

Little Pigeon Creek sign located at the point where Route 162 crosses over the creek a short distance from the Lincoln farm site.

The half-faced story began with the writings of William H. Herndon and soon found its way into subsequent biographies. The tale is likely fiction, however, as Abraham Lincoln himself reveals in his biographical comments to John Locke Scripps in June of 1860: "From this place [Kentucky] he [Abraham Lincoln] removed to what is now Spencer County, Indiana, in the autumn of 1816, Abraham then being in his eighth year. ... A few days before completion of his eighth year, in the absence of his father, a flock of wild turkeys approached the *new log cabin* [emphasis added], and Abraham with a rifle-gun, standing inside, shot through a crack and killed one of them."

Here Lincoln tells us that in early February the cabin was completed, referring to it as "the new log cabin." In 1865 John Hanks gave an interview in which he stated that it took only four days to construct the log home at Decatur, Illinois, a typical time frame for skilled cabin builders. One account recorded by a neighbor of Thomas Lincoln read, "Arrived on Tuesday, cut logs for the cabin on Wednesday, raised the cabin on Thursday, clap boards from an old sugar camp put on Friday and on Saturday made the crude furniture to go to housekeeping."

Clearly, an experienced woodsman like Thomas Lincoln, with the help of his neighbors, could have erected their new log home in only a few days after arriving in the autumn of 1816. Certainly by February, the family was moved into their new home, belying the image that it took Thomas Lincoln a year to build a home for his family.

Indiana proved to be richer farmland than Kentucky and, with dense forests of hardwood, provided well for the new settlers. While both Kentucky and Ohio had populations numbering five hundred thousand, Indiana was still considerably sparser, numbering only sixty-five thousand. Even so, the new home was close to seven other families, was within walking distance of the village of Gentryville, and only seventeen miles from the county seat of Rockport located on the Ohio River.

If Kentucky gave birth to Lincoln, Indiana raised him to manhood. For fourteen years, from age seven through twenty-one, Lincoln lived a Hoosier

The muddy waters of Little Pigeon Creek, following a heavy downpour of rain.

among the forests of the country's westernmost edge. Within a few days of his settling along Little Pigeon Creek, Indiana joined the Union as the nineteenth state. Fortunately for Thomas Lincoln and his son, it joined as a free state. The new constitution banned slavery, yet left in place one hundred ninety slaves that existed at the time Indiana adopted its constitution. By 1830, the number had dropped to three.

It was while living in Indiana that Lincoln would write his first letter, read his first newspaper, give his first public speech, travel away from home for the first time, and get into his first fight. Here he would fell his first tree, split his first rail, and plough his first furrow; and it would be in Indiana where he would experience his first of several tragedies.

The fall of 1818 saw an epidemic spread across southern Indiana. The local people referred to it as the "milk sickness" because of their belief that it was contracted by drinking the milk of cows that had become infected by eating a plant known as "snakeroot." This weed grew predominately in the understory of the shaded forest, and as cattle depleted their pastures they moved into the wooded areas for forage. Here they found large amounts of the poisonous plant that supplemented their diet.

In early fall, Thomas and Elizabeth Hanks Sparrow, Nancy Lincoln's aunt and uncle who had emigrated to Indiana a year after Thomas Lincoln and his family, came down with the illness. Within a few days they were both dead, leaving nineteen-year-old Dennis Hanks, who lived with them, an orphan. Dennis moved in with Thomas and Nancy and their two young children. Within days the dreaded illness struck Nancy. As the days passed it

The Indiana Cabin

All the Lincoln cabins were newly constructed by Thomas Lincoln with the help of family and friends. Because Lincoln was a skilled cabinetmaker and expert woodsman, the cabins he built were of high quality. The Indiana cabin shown below is constructed in the style typical of those built on the early frontier. The size of these cabins was twenty feet in length by eighteen feet in width, requiring approximately forty logs. The logs were squared (hewed) on all four sides and notched at the ends to fit close together. The openings between the logs were filled with moistened clay to form a tight seal. Accounts from the period indicate that a log cabin of the type the Lincolns lived in could be built in four to five days. The replica cabin below, built in 1968, is located at the living historical farm, Lincoln Boyhood National Memorial, Lincoln City, Indiana.

Thomas stakes a claim.

On May 1, 1816, the vast government lands in the Indiana Territory were placed on sale. Nearly a thousand tracts were sold at an average price of $3.00 an acre. In the fall of that same year Thomas Lincoln journeyed to southern Indiana in search of a new farm. After years of trouble with land titles in Kentucky he knew the government surveys in Indiana were reliable. He selected a quarter section of 160 acres in Perry County (later Spencer County) and staked out his claim. By the time he returned with his family several weeks later, Indiana had become the nineteenth state in the Union with a population of just over 65,000.

A view of the farm from the cabin.

The rear of the replica cabin.

The shed containing many of the tools necessary to maintain a working farm.

The Lincolns at Home

Diorama depicting a traditional view of the Lincoln family in their Indiana home. A young Abraham reads by the light of the cabin's fireplace while his stepmother, Sarah Bush Lincoln, sits knitting and his father stands in the doorway. The family dog sits by Lincoln. Missing from the scene is Lincoln's sister, Sarah, two years his senior. Also missing are Sarah Bush Lincoln's three children from her previous marriage and Dennis Hanks, Lincoln's cousin.

By all accounts the cabin was well furnished and comfortable, although somewhat crowded, housing eight people. The cabin measured approximately twenty feet by eighteen feet and was constructed of hewn logs. The two windows located on either side of the door are accurate according to photographs taken after Lincoln's assassination.

Diorama in Chicago Historical Society.

became obvious that Nancy was dying too. According to Dennis Hanks, Nancy called the young children to her bedside and "told them to be good & kind to their father – to one another and to the world, expressing a hope that they might live as they had been taught by her to love man, reverence and worship God." Dennis was attempting to put a good light on the tragedy. On October 5, 1818, Nancy died, leaving young Abraham and his eleven-year-old sister, Sarah, without the caring and tender hand of their mother.

Thomas Lincoln used his carpentry skills to fashion three coffins from whipsawed boards while young Abraham helped by whittling wooden pegs to hold the boards in place. While nails existed, they were rare and hence quite valuable. Wooden pegs were perfectly adequate for binding coffin boards together. The grieving family buried the young mother on a gentle rise of land a few hundred feet from the cabin in a grove of trees where the woods were cool and shaded. No formal service was read over the grave, there being no regular minister available at the time.

A year later the Lincolns' Kentucky pastor, Reverend David Elkins, passed through the area, visiting his Indiana relatives. To young Abraham's delight he stopped by the Lincoln cabin and performed the burial service for Nancy, according to the Baptist liturgy.

In 1819, Thomas Lincoln bid his children and Dennis Hanks goodbye and headed back to Elizabethtown and the home of the widow Sarah Bush Johnston. Thomas had once courted Sarah Bush, but lost out to Daniel Johnston. Sarah Bush married Johnston and together they had three children, two girls and a boy. A few months before the Lincoln family left Kentucky for Indiana, Daniel Johnston died, leaving Sarah a widow with three young children. Nancy Hanks had known the Johnstons and Nancy and Sarah were friends, both giving birth to baby girls around the same time.

Thomas visited Sarah in her Elizabethtown cabin and pointed out to her that they both had lost their partners and were with young children. He asked her to marry him and join him in Indiana, bringing the children together – his with a new mother, hers with a new father. According to her family's tradition, Sarah said she was willing, but had several small debts that she had to pay before marrying and moving to Indiana. Thomas asked for a list and by evening had visited Sarah's creditors and paid them off.

Sarah Bush Johnston and Thomas Lincoln were married on December 2, 1819, in the cabin of Reverend George L. Rodgers, which stood next door to Sarah Johnston's cabin. Thomas secured a wagon and horses from his brother-in-law, Ralph Crume, who was married to his older sister Mary. He put Sarah and her three children, Elizabeth, Matilda, and John, into the wagon, along with Sarah's substantial household goods, and headed back to Indiana.

A city girl all her life, Sarah recalled her first impressions of her new home to William Herndon in 1865. "When we landed in Indiana Mr Lincoln had erected a good log cabin tolerably Comfortable. ... The country was wild – and desolate." Sarah set about immediately to restore cleanliness and order to both the cabin and its inhabitants. Herndon later wrote that "she soaped, rubbed, and washed the children clean, so that they looked pretty, neat, well & clean. She sewed and mended their clothes & the children once more looked human as their own good mother left them." Testimony from several family members attests to Sarah's kind and thoughtful treatment of all five children. From the day of her arrival she accepted all five as her own and never showed the slightest distinction between them. Abraham and John were treated alike as were Sarah, Elizabeth and Matilda. Years later Lincoln reflected on his stepmother: "She took the children and mixed us up together like hasty pudding, and has not known us apart since."

Top: Interior of the replica cabin. Note the peg ladder to the left of the fireplace leading up to the loft.

Right: A corner cabinet copied after an original cabinet made by Thomas Lincoln.

While Sarah carefully raised her children with an even hand, she recognized from the very first that Abraham was different, special, and she felt a special bond between herself and her new son. Years later, after his death, she told Herndon:

> Abe was a good boy, and I can say what scarcely one woman, a mother, can say in a thousand and it is this: Abe never gave me a cross word or look and never refused in fact, or even in appearance, to do anything I requested him. I never gave him a cross word in all my life. He was kind to everybody and to everything and always accommodated others if he could. ... He was dutiful to me always; he loved me truly, I think. I had a son John who was raised with Abe. Both were good boys, but I must say, both now being dead, that Abe was the best boy I ever saw or ever expect to see.

Although Sarah could neither read nor write, she was a strong advocate of Abraham's learning. Knowing her new son's passion for learning, she helped him in every manner possible, including the enlisting of her husband's support. Thomas Lincoln did not object to young Abraham's passion, except when it continued to get in the way of those tasks which had to be done. "As a usual thing, Mr. Lincoln never made Abe quit reading to do anything if he could avoid it. He would do it himself first. ... [H]e himself felt the uses and necessities of education and wanted his boy Abraham to learn and he encouraged him to do it in all ways he could," Sarah would state. And again, "Old Tom couldn't read himself, but he wuz proud that Abe could, and many a time he'd brag about how smart Abe wuz to folks around about."

In 1822, at the ages of thirteen and fifteen, Abraham and Sarah attended James Sweeney's (sometimes spelled Swaney's) "Blab" school located four miles from their home. They attended the school for no more than four months. Two years later, the two continued their sparse schooling at the school of Azel Dorsey. It was at the time Lincoln attended Dorsey's school that he clearly developed his skills at writing and penmanship and wrote out the little doggerel that survives today as his earliest known writing:

Abraham Lincoln
his hand and pen.
he will be good but
god knows When

This doggerel is indicative of Lincoln's fascination with and love of poetry. Over the next three decades he composed several poems to express his feelings about certain subjects that moved him. Fourteen years after he had left Indiana, Lincoln returned on a political expedition on behalf of Henry Clay. He visited his old neighborhood and those of his old friends who were still alive and living there. In 1846, some eighteen months after his return, he penned a twenty-one-stanza poem consisting of two cantos and the beginning of a third:

> *My childhood home I see again,*
> *and gladden with the view;*
> *And still as mem'ries crowd my brain,*
> *there's sadness in it too.*
>
> *O memory! thou mid-way world*
> *'Twixt Earth and Paradise,*
> *Where things decayed, and loved ones lost*
> *In dreamy shadows rise.*

And further on:

> *Now twenty years have passed away,*
> *Since here I bid farewell*
> *To woods, and fields, and scenes of play*
> *And school-mates loved so well.*
>
> *Where many were, how few remain*
> *Of old familiar things!*
> *But seeing these to mind again*
> *The lost and absent brings.*
>
> *The friends I left that parting day –*
> *How changed, as time has sped!*
> *Young childhood grown, strong manhood grey,*
> *And half of all are dead.*
>
> *I hear the lone survivors tell*
> *How nought from death could save,*
> *Til every sound appears a knell,*
> *And every spot a grave.*
>
> *I range the fields with pensive tread,*
> *And pace the hollow rooms;*
> *And feel companions of the dead*
> *I'm living in the tombs.*

LINES WRITTEN BY LINCOLN ON THE LEAF OF HIS SCHOOL-BOOK
IN HIS FOURTEENTH YEAR.
Preserved by his Step-mother.
Original in possession of J. W. Weik.

Caption from doggerel at left. Source: Gutenberg.org

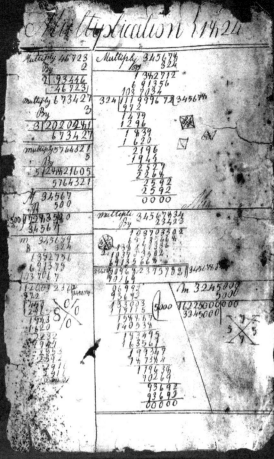

According to Lincoln's stepmother, Lincoln had a copy book during the few months he attended school in Indiana. Thomas Johnston had possession of the book in the years following Lincoln's death. In 1866, the copy book passed to William Herndon who dispensed the pages to various friends. Twelve of the separated pages survive, dating from 1824 and 1826 when Lincoln was fifteen and seventeen years old. The surviving pages cover various exercises on mathematics, including simple interest, land and dry measures, long division and multiplication.
Source: Columbia University.

"Boyhood of Lincoln"
by Eastman Johnson, 1868
Source: Wikimedia Commons

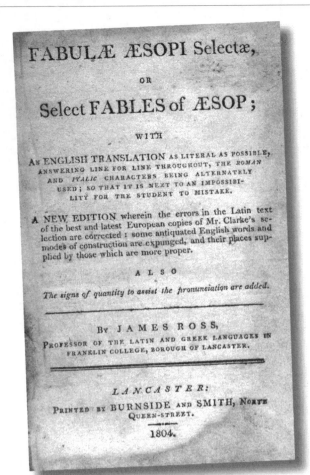

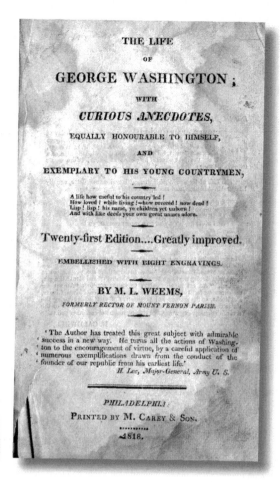

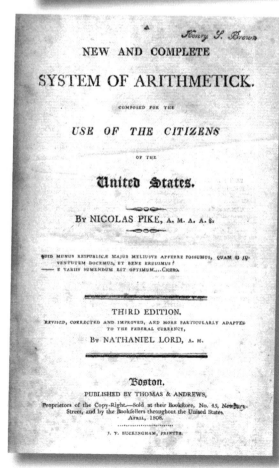

While books were a rare item on the early frontier, Abraham Lincoln seemed particularly adept at seeking out and finding a sufficient number of copies to satisfy his thirst for knowledge. While Lincoln was not a voracious reader, he did read extensively from books he was able to find from among his neighbors. Throughout his life he chose his reading materials selectively and retained most everything he read.

Among the first books to come into his possession after the Bible were two shown here: *Aesop's Fables* and Weem's *Life of George Washington*. From one neighbor, David Turnham, a farmer and justice of the peace, Lincoln borrowed the *Revised Laws of Indiana*. The book contained copies of the Declaration of Independence and the Constitution, which were undoubtedly the first copies Lincoln read. Lincoln borrowed the *Life of George Washington* from another neighbor, Josiah Crawford. The book became damaged when Lincoln absentmindedly left it out in the rain. Lincoln agreed to reimburse Crawford for the book by pulling fodder for him for two days.

Years later while riding the circuit as a lawyer Lincoln secured a copy of Euclid's *Elements* and set about mastering many of the mathematician's postulates and theorems, a difficult feat for most.

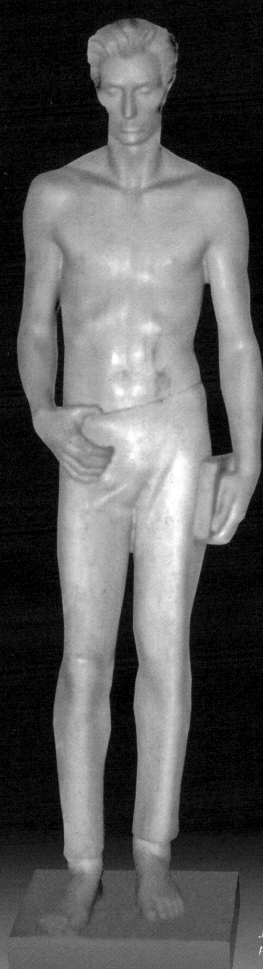

"Young Lincoln"

In 1939, James Hansen, a twenty-one-year-old art student, entered a Works Progress Administration competition for paintings and sculptures designed for use in Federal buildings. Using himself as the model, Hansen entered his model of a youthful Lincoln dressed only in a pair of breeches and holding a book. Selected as one of the winning entries, Hansen was awarded $7,200 to carve an heroic limestone replica of his model for the Los Angeles Federal Courthouse (formerly the Los Angeles Post Office and Courthouse).

    Originally displayed in the Corcoran Gallery of Art in 1939, following its display at the New York World's Fair, the plaster model used as Hansen's entry was later moved to the lobby of the District of Columbia Recorder of Deeds Building on its completion in 1941.

The Fine Arts Section of the U.S. Department of the Treasury commissioned this 8-foot sculpture *Young Lincoln* by James Hansen (1917-) in 1939 based on an open and anonymous competition available to all sculptors west of the Mississippi for the decoration of the Los Angeles Post Office and Courthouse lobby. "Young Lincoln" was exhibited in the Works Progress Administration Building of the 1939 New York World's Fair and was installed in its present location in 1941. It was Hansen's first large-scale sculpture, and the artist used himself as the model for the gangly figure of Lincoln. Hansen developed his own interpretation of Lincoln, portraying him as a young man standing barefoot and shirtless – a man of deep sentiment and understanding.

James Lee Hansen's life-sized plaster statue, "Young Lincoln."

Young Lincoln at Work

Young Lincoln filled most of his days for the next few years with the routine of hard farm work. Ploughing and cultivating fields, felling trees, splitting rails, and being hired out by his father to neighbors where he not only earned money for his father, but gained access to his neighbors' libraries. In 1825, at the age of sixteen, he was hired by James Taylor to help run a ferryboat across the Ohio River from the mouth of Anderson Creek to the Kentucky side. It was as a result of his exposure to the ferry business, and his own entrepreneurial ambitions, that Lincoln found himself in trouble with the law.

During his days with Taylor, Lincoln built himself a small skiff and occasionally ferried passengers out to passing steamboats. After one such trip in which he carried two men to a waiting steamer in midstream, the two men each tossed a silver half dollar into the bottom of Lincoln's skiff after he deposited them on the boat. Lincoln was overwhelmed by the fact that he had earned a whole dollar for less than a day's work. Soon thereafter, another ferryman, by the name of John Dill, on behalf of his brother Lyn and himself, took Lincoln before a Kentucky Justice of the Peace, Samuel Pate, for operating a ferry without a license. Pate, the original builder and owner of the Elizabethtown cabin in which Thomas and Sarah had married in 1819, ruled that ferrying passengers to mid-stream did not constitute "setting them over" and therefore Lincoln did not violate the statute. He was acquitted, to his glee. The experience, however, sparked an interest in the law that would soon consume him.

> *You may think it was a very little thing, but it was a most important incident in my life. I could scarcely believe that I, a poor boy, had earned a dollar in less than a day. The world seemed wider and fairer before me. I was a more hopeful and confident being from that time.*
>
> A. Lincoln
> to William Seward

Lincoln, now a young man of nineteen, suffered a second tragic setback when his only sister, Sarah, died unexpectedly during childbirth. The wife of Aaron Grigsby, Sarah gave birth to a stillborn baby and died soon after. Lincoln was grief-stricken and bitter, blaming Grigsby for neglect by not acting sooner to help Sarah. In the space of ten years, young Lincoln lost two of the most important women in his life and felt their loss deeply. His melancholy only deepened after Sarah's death.

Lincoln explained his own feelings years later in a letter to a young twenty-year-old girl who had lost her father in the Civil War:

> In this sad world of ours, sorrow comes to all; and to the young, it comes with bitterest agony, because it takes them unawares. The older have learned to ever expect it. ... Perfect relief is not possible except with time. ... You are sure to be happy again. To know this, which is certainly true, will make you some less miserable now. I have had experience enough to know what I say; and you need only to believe it, to feel better at once.

In April 1828, Lincoln was offered the chance of his young life. James Gentry, founder of the small town of Gentryville and proprietor of the store there, hired Lincoln to accompany Gentry's son Allen to pilot a flatboat to New Orleans. Gentry paid Lincoln the great sum of eight dollars a month from the time the trip started until Lincoln arrived back home, a generous arrangement by any standard. Lincoln accepted and the two youths set off down the Ohio for the Mississippi and New Orleans.

The trip was a major learning experience for the young man. Never had he seen or experienced such sights or sounds or smells. On entering the Mississippi, they began trading their cargo for tobacco, sugar, and cotton. Tying up overnight near a large plantation at Baton Rouge, the two men were attacked by a gang of seven blacks who had observed the pair during the day. The blacks had thought of easily overpowering the two, killing them, and after tossing their bodies overboard, stealing the cargo. Fortunately for the two youths, and the future country, Lincoln and Gentry fought off the seven attackers and tossed all seven in the Mississippi. Free from immediate danger, they untied their raft and quickly proceeded downriver to New Orleans.

It was at New Orleans that Lincoln had his first experience with the horror of slavery. According to Allen Gentry, "We stood and watched slaves sold in New Orleans and Abraham became very angry." After disposing of their remaining goods and the flatboat, the two men boarded a steamer and headed back up the river, eventually debarking at Rockport a few miles south of home.

Abraham Lincoln
The Rail Fence Builder
by Louis Slobodkin (1939)

Winner of a national competition sponsored by the Works Progress Administration, sculptor Louis Slobodkin was commissioned by the U.S. government to produce a fifteen-foot plaster model of his young Abraham Lincoln to accompany the U.S. exhibit at the 1939 New York World's Fair. After its completion and erection in the Garden Court of the U.S. Pavillion, the plaster statue was ordered destroyed by Edward J. Flynn, commissioner of the fair, when members of the congressional delegation "scoffed at it" as being disgraceful. During the night, before the fair was to open, work crews were sent in and broke the statue into pieces, hauling it away. In reaching a settlement following his lawsuit, Slobodkin cast a seven-and-a-half-foot bronze statue that was exhibited at the Corcoran Gallery of Art before being permanently displayed in the courtyard of the Department of the Interior, Washington, D.C. The strange story of Slobodkin and his statue that stands hidden from public view has faded from public memory.

U.S. Department of the Interior

A. Lincoln, ferry boatman, becomes A. Lincoln, defendant.

LINCOLN ACQUITTED

Abraham Lincoln, 16th president of United States, won his first law case here, 1827. Charged by the Commonwealth of Kentucky with operating ferry without license; Lincoln pleaded his own case in trial at the home of presiding Justice of the Peace, Samuel Pate. Pate encouraged Lincoln to study law and loaned him books. Lincoln often visited here on "law days."

Ferryman John Dill sued Lincoln for operating a ferry without a license. The case was heard before Justice of the Peace Samuel Pate. Lincoln won.

A houseboat anchored at a point where Anderson Creek empties into the Ohio River. It was from this point that Lincoln ferried individuals to steamboats waiting in midstream. Photograph ca. 1910. From R. Gerald McMurtry, "The Lincoln Migration from Kentucky to Indiana," *Indiana Magazine of History,* vol. 33, no. 4 (December 1937).

In 1825, at the age of sixteen, Lincoln hired out to James Taylor who lived near the spot where the Anderson Creek emptied into the Ohio River. Taylor operated a ferry among his many enterprises and hired young Lincoln to help run the ferry. The river was only one hundred feet wide at Taylor's ferry crossing but nearly fifteen feet in depth. During his employment, Lincoln lived at the Taylor house.

While employed by Taylor and living in his house, Lincoln built a small skiff that he kept at the landing. One day two well-dressed men approached Lincoln and asked if he would row them to the steamboat at anchor in the middle of the river. Lincoln agreed and after delivering the two men to the steamboat they each tossed a silver half-dollar into Lincoln's boat in payment for the trip. Lincoln was dumbfounded. Years later he recounted his experience:

> I could scarcely believe my eyes. You may think it was a very little thing, but it was a most important incident in my life. I could scarcely believe that I, a poor boy, had earned a dollar in less than a day. The world seemed wider and fairer before me. I was a more hopeful and confident being from that time.

Enthused by his newly discovered enterprise, Lincoln began offering his small service to others in need of ferrying to waiting steamboats. The venture, however, landed Lincoln in court. Two brothers, who lived on the Kentucky side of the river and operated a ferry service under a franchise licensed by the state, had Lincoln brought before Justice of the Peace Samuel Pate for operating a ferry without a license. The law stated:

> If any person set any person over any river or creek, whereupon public ferries are appointed, he or she shall forfeit and pay five pounds current money, for every such offense, one moiety to the ferry-keeper nearest the place where such offense shall be committed, the other moiety to the informer; and if such ferry-keeper informs, he shall have the whole penalty.

Justice Pate agreed with the defendant that Lincoln had not infringed on the ferrymen because the law only referred to putting passengers across the river and not to a midpoint in the river. Lincoln was acquitted of the charge.

Lincoln had experienced his first taste of the law and liked what he experienced. He became keenly interested in the legal profession and set about learning all he could. From his neighbor David Turnham he obtained a copy of the *Revised Laws of Indiana,* to which were prefixed the Declaration of Independence, the Constitution of the United States, the Constitution of the State of Indiana, and sundry other documents connected with the political history of the Territory and State of Indiana.

I could scarcely believe that I, a poor boy, had earned a dollar in less than a day.
A. Lincoln

Lincoln in his small skiff examining the two silver half-dollars he earned rowing two men to a waiting steamboat in the Ohio River.

Samuel Pate House, Lewisport, Kentucky. Lincoln was tried before Justice of the Peace Samuel Pate in this house for infringing on another ferryman's franchise. The case was dismissed.
From a postcard (date unknown). Courtesy of Joseph E. Garrera.

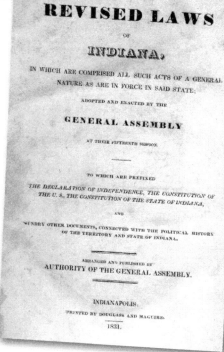

Lincoln received a copy of the Revised Laws of Indiana *(1824 edition) from his friend and neighbor, David Turnham. The Turnham family lived less than a mile from the Lincoln farm.*

A Great Adventure:
Abe Lincoln Goes Flatboating.

When he was 19, still residing in Indiana, he made his first trip upon a flat-boat to New Orleans.
He was a hired-hand merely, and he and the son of the owner without other assistance, made the trip.

A. Lincoln, autobiography written for John L. Scripps, June 1860.

In 1828, the same year as the tragic death of his sister, Abraham Lincoln set out on the first great adventure of his life. James Gentry, a local merchant and store owner, hired Lincoln to help Gentry's son, Allen, take a cargo of goods down the Mississippi River to New Orleans. It was fall and the abundance of the summer's harvest would turn a handsome profit for James Gentry when sold in the bustling commerce of the old French city. Because most of the trade at Gentry's store was through barter, he was left at the end of the growing season with a large surplus of produce.

It was this surplus that he needed to send down the river to New Orleans where he could turn it into capital. Gentry paid Lincoln eight dollars a month plus his return passage on one of the hundreds of steamboats that plied the waters of the Mississippi.

New Orleans was the fifth largest city in the United States at the time. Its population of 46,000 was an exotic mix of new world and old world culture and to the young Lincoln it was worlds apart from the backwoods of Kentucky and Indiana. It was the first of two trips that Lincoln would make down the great river. Together, the trips would total over 2,500 miles and take Lincoln to places he had only dreamed of as a young boy.

The point of departure was the small town of Rockport, the county seat of Spencer County. Originally called Hanging Rock, Rockport was located on a low cliff overlooking the Ohio River sixteen miles from the cabin of Thomas Lincoln. The population of the small town was just over one hundred people.

Lincoln and Allen Gentry were hired to build the flatboat they would use to travel to New Orleans. While the exact dimensions of their flatboat are not known, the details of similar flatboats can be found in courthouse records of the period. One such contract describes a flatboat constructed to haul goods to New Orleans. It was sixty-five feet in length, eighteen feet wide with two foot gunnels nine inches thick. The boat was built at the riverside bottom side up until the gunnels were attached, then turned over with the help of oxen and floated in the river to test its worthiness.

Leaving Rockport on December 18, Lincoln and Gentry made their way down the Ohio River into the Mississippi without incident. Sixty miles above New Orleans the two men encountered a near tragic event. After securing their barge along the river bank for the night the pair was attacked by seven black men intent on killing them and stealing their cargo. Years later Lincoln described the event in the third person as he often did: "One night they were attacked by seven negroes with intent to kill and rob them. They were hurt some in the melee, but succeeded in driving the negroes from the boat, and then 'cut cable,' 'weighed anchor' and left." The attack could have easily gone against the pair with tragic results for both men and for the future of the nation.

Map: Library of Congress

New Orleans presented a new world to the young Lincoln. He witnessed the multicultural diversity found in few other places. Sights, sounds, and smells previously unknown. Among the more disturbing sights were the numerous slave auctions taking place. Years later, Absalom, Allen Gentry's son, claimed that his father told him, "We stood and watched the slaves sold in New Orleans and Abraham became very angry."

Lincoln and Gentry returned home on one of the numerous steamboats that worked the river. They had been gone for two months. In that short period of time they witnessed a slice of civilization most of their peers never experienced in a lifetime. It was the beginning of an education that would serve Lincoln well in his future journey. A few weeks before the start of their trip Lincoln celebrated his twentieth birthday. He was one year away from his legal majority, and the trip to New Orleans was the beginning of his independence that would soon take place.

Slave Auction

Among the many sights Lincoln saw in New Orleans was the public auction of slaves. Years later, Allen Gentry told his son Absalom, "We stood and watched the slaves sold in New Orleans and Abraham was very angry." Such reminiscences were also claimed following Lincoln's 1830 flatboat trip to New Orleans. Whether any of them were true or not, Lincoln saw the business of slavery and its effect marked him deeply. Chicago Historical Society

Abraham Lincoln, Flatboatman

Lincoln made two trips down the Mississippi River to New Orleans. Both trips were by flatboats he helped construct, hauling goods for merchants that hired him to carry them to market. The first trip occurred in 1828 and left from Rockport, Indiana. The second occurred in 1830 and left from Springfield, Illinois. On both trips Lincoln witnessed the sale of slaves. The experience affected him such that he would later state, "If slavery is not wrong, then nothing is wrong." Etching by Alfred Waud.

The Father of Waters

Like a giant tree whose outstretched limbs form an enormous canopy, the Mississippi River and its tributaries link over sixty percent of the contiguous United States. Beginning in Lake Itasca in northwest Minnesota, the river traverses 2,340 miles before emptying into the Gulf of Mexico, or if measured from the headwaters of the Missouri River, 3,765 miles. The distance by water from Rockport, where Lincoln's journey began, to New Orleans was just over 1,200 miles and took the two young men two months to complete. It was the adventure of a lifetime and the imprint made by the mighty river stuck with Lincoln his entire life.

The winding river made so many twists and turns that over a stretch of only twenty miles it flowed in all four directions: east, south, west, and north. To travel twenty miles as the crow flies would require traversing sixty miles by water.

The number of vessels of all types plying the river was huge. In 1828, New Orleans recorded 750 steamboat arrivals and over 1,000 flatboats. One New Orleans newspaper noted that on a single day in 1828 there were docked in her harbor sixty-six ships, eighty-five brigs, thirty schooners, six sloops, and twenty steamboats. On the same day several hundred flatboats were crammed into every nook and cranny of her port.

In July of 1863 when the cities of Vicksburg and Port Hudson surrendered to Union forces, Lincoln poetically mused that "the Father of Waters flows unvexed to the sea." Lincoln knew better than most that control of the Mississippi River was the key to Confederate defeat. The river was the very lifeblood of Confederate independence.

Is This Woman Lincoln's Beloved Stepmother?

Traditional image of Sarah Lincoln. Stephenson County Historical Society, Freeport, Illinois.

Discovered in the Stephenson County, Illinois, Historical Society's collection after going unnoticed for nearly fifty years, this photograph is only the second known image of Sarah Bush Johnston Lincoln. The photograph is described as an ambrotype and probably dates from the 1860s. Stephenson County Historical Society, Freeport, Illinois.

History is replete with serendipitous discoveries that help enrich our understanding of the past. On a crisp November morning in November, Civil War enthusiast and historian Joe Grove made a startling discovery while visiting the Stephenson County Historical Society. Among the displays was an image of an elderly woman that caught Mr. Grove's attention. Having researched images believed to be of Sarah Bush Johnston Lincoln, Grove later stated, "The sight of the portrait stopped me in my tracks." Gaining permission to examine the image more closely, Grove removed it from its handsome case. Written on the inside paper backing of the case was an inscription that read, "Sally Bush Abraham Lincolns Stepmother and Thomas Lincolns second wife." The fact that Sarah was referred to as "Sally" is important to the discovery. Sally was the nickname Sarah Lincoln was known by only among family members and close friends. Lincoln was known to have referred to his stepmother as "Aunt Sally." Wayne Temple, Chief Deputy Director of the Illinois State Archives, wrote, "Since only close family members would have called the subject "Sally," there can be little doubt that it is a genuine picture of Lincoln's beloved stepmother." Unlike the traditional photograph of Sarah Lincoln, the Stephenson portrait is not retouched and is more lifelike.

Sarah would talk extensively of those first Indiana years and of her illustrious stepson to William Herndon, Lincoln's law partner and early biographer.

"When I arrived in Indianny those two children were a pitiable sight. A good scrubbing of both of them along with their humble cabin soon set things right. Tom had been most neglectful."

"Abe was a good boy; he didn't like physical labor, but was diligent for knowledge, He read all the books he could lay his hands on, and when he came across a passage that struck him, he would write it down on a board if he had no paper, and keep it there till he did get paper, then he would rewrite it, look at it, and repeat it until he fixed it in his mind."

"He had a small copybook, a kind of scrapbook, in which he put down all things and that way preserved them you see."

"Abe had no particular religion to speak of. Least ways he never talked about it. On Sundays, however, he would hear sermons by our Baptist preacher, come home, take the other children out, climb up on a stump, and almost repeat the sermon word for word. The children would all laugh. It was great fun for them. Me and Tom marveled at his mind."

"Abe was a moderate eater, and I now have no remembrance of his special dish; although he did seem partial to gingerbread."

"He sat down and ate what was set before him, making no complaints; he seemed careless about this. I cooked his meals for nearly fifteen years. He always had good health, never was sick, was very careful of his person, was tolerably neat and clean - only he cared nothing for clothes. He didn't wear clothes, rather clothes hung on him like on a rack."

"Abe was a good boy, and I can say what scarcely one mother in a thousand can say, and it is this: Abe never gave me a cross word or look and never refused to do anything I requested of him. I never gave him a cross word in all my life. His mind and mine, what little I had, seemed to run together in the same channel."

"He was here after he was elected President of the United States." (Here the old lady stopped, turned around and sobbed, wiped her eyes, and proceeded.)

"I did not want Abe to run for President - did not want him elected. I was afraid somehow or other - felt it in my heart that something would happen to him, and when he came down to see me after he was elected President, I still felt in my heart that something would befall Abe and that I should never see again."

Life-like figure of the young teenage Lincoln displayed in the Abraham Lincoln Presidential Museum and Library in Springfield, Illinois.

Sarah Bush Johnston Lincoln
1788-1869

Sarah Bush Johnston Lincoln was the daughter of Christopher Bush, the grandson of a Dutch immigrant from Rotterdam who first settled in New York. She was known among family members as "Sally" to distinguish her from her stepdaughter, Sarah Lincoln. Sarah Bush was born December 13, 1788, the youngest of nine children born to Hanna and Christopher Bush. According to Louis A. Warren, first director of the Lincoln Library and Museum in Fort Wayne, Indiana, Thomas Lincoln and Sarah Bush were romantically involved as young people in early Elizabethtown. For whatever reason, Sarah decided to marry Daniel Johnston while Thomas and Sarah's brother Isaac were on a boat trip to New Orleans.

Having failed to woo Sarah, Thomas returned to the Beech Fork community in Washington County and courted Nancy Hanks who he had known for many years. The couple were married on June 12, 1806, and returned to his farm on Mill Creek in Hardin County before settling in their Elizabethtown cabin.

Sarah's original choice was a poor one as Daniel Johnston was constantly in debt, relying on family members to bail him out. When Johnston died in 1815, Sarah was saddled with her profligate husband's debts.

Sarah and Daniel had three children, two girls named Elizabeth and Matilda, and a younger boy named John D. Johnston. John would acquire his father's ways in later life and spend a good part of it in debt, often asking his stepbrother, Abraham, to lend him money.

Sarah somehow acquired a cabin in Elizabethtown from Samuel Haycraft for the modest sum of twenty-five dollars, where she moved her young family. It is this Elizabethtown cabin that is often confused in the early literature as the birth cabin of Abraham Lincoln.

Thomas Lincoln was living at Knob Creek in the Elizabethtown area when Daniel Johnston died in 1815. He moved his family to Indiana one year later. Nancy Lincoln died in 1818, leaving Thomas a widower with two young children. Ten months later, Thomas returned to Elizabethtown and proposed marriage to Sarah. Still saddled with her husband's debts, Thomas agreed to pay them off, thus freeing Sarah of her obligation. They were married on December 2, 1819, spending the next thirty-two years together in Indiana and Illinois. Thomas died in 1851, age sixty-three. Sarah died December 10, 1869, three days shy of her eighty-first birthday. Sarah Bush Lincoln is buried next to her husband in the Shiloh Baptist Cemetery near Charleston, Illinois.

Cabin depicted in an early postcard, believed by present-day historians to be the home of Sarah Bush Johnston in Elizabethtown.

A New Life in a New World

Fourteen months after the death of Nancy Lincoln, Thomas Lincoln left twelve-year-old Sarah and ten-year-old Abraham with their cousin Dennis Hanks, now twenty years old, and returned to Kentucky to ask Sarah Bush Johnston to become his wife and his children's new mother.

While several versions of the story of Thomas Lincoln's proposal to Sarah Johnston exist, that of Sarah's brother, Isaac Bush, is believed closest to the truth. According to this nephew, Thomas Lincoln called on Sarah one day and pointed out that they had known each other for several years and both were now without their spouses. Both had young children and both needed the other. Thomas then asked Sarah to marry him and return with him to Indiana. Sarah demurred, stating that she owed several small debts that she felt she had to pay before leaving town. "Thomas Lincoln asked her how much they were, and after learning, went out and paid off each of them and they were married."

Thomas was forty-one and Sarah was thirty-one years old at the time. Following the marriage, Thomas obtained a wagon from his brother-in-law, Ralph Crume, and packed Sarah's belongings and her three children into the wagon and returned to his home in Indiana, where he had left his two children in the care of Dennis Hanks.

Marriage bond in the "just and full sum of fifty pounds United States currency." According to to Kentucky law at the time, the bond was required in order to secure a marriage license.

Marriage license authorizing any "minister of the gospel or authorized magistrate to join together in the honorable state of matrimony Mr. Thomas Lincoln and Miss Sarah Johnston." Both documents on file in the Hardin County Courthouse, Elizabethtown, Kentucky.

Thomas Lincoln's Indiana Cabin

Much of Abraham Lincoln's early life is built around oral tradition. Two individuals account for most of what we accept: Dennis Hanks and William Herndon. Hanks holds a special place in the Lincoln story because he was contemporary with Lincoln and grew up living part of his youth with the Lincoln family; Herndon, Lincoln's close friend and law partner, because he set out shortly after Lincoln's death to document as much of Lincoln's early life as he could. He did this not through research into primary documents, but by interviewing people who knew Lincoln and had lived part of their lives along with his. Both individuals suffer from the challenge of time, relying on data gleaned as much as fifty years after the fact. While oral history and tradition have value to an historian, it is generally fraught with difficulty. Faulty memories are too often enhanced by what people have read or heard years later, which inevitably become a part of the story. Separating fact from fiction becomes the primary job of every historian and herein lies the problem.

While William Herndon had great respect for the truth and worked diligently to gather the true story of his famous partner, he suffered from his own prejudices. In his attempt to elevate Lincoln, he chose to denigrate Lincoln's early life. The more deprived and hardscrabble the young Lincoln's life was the more remarkable his rise to greatness. At the same time, Herndon's dislike, some would say hatred, of Mary Lincoln, Lincoln's wife, led Herndon to distort the very history he was attempting to uncover. A case in point is Herndon's account of the "half-faced camp" Thomas Lincoln built for his family on arriving in Indiana.

Herndon, in his three-volume biography of Lincoln, described the scene of the Lincoln family's arrival in Indiana. It was in December 1816 that Thomas Lincoln arrived at his Indiana site. The weather was cold and unwelcoming to the small family, and Thomas set about providing shelter.

The structure when completed was fourteen feet square, and was built of small unhewn logs. In the language of the day, it was called a "half-faced camp," and enclosed on all sides but one. It had neither floor, door, nor windows. In this forbidding hovel these doughty emigrants braved the exposure of the varying seasons for *an entire year* [emphasis added]. At the end of that time Thomas and Betsy Sparrow followed, bringing with them Dennis Hanks; and to them Thomas Lincoln surrendered the "half-faced camp," while he moved into a more pretentious structure – a cabin enclosed on all sides.

Herndon relied entirely on Dennis Hanks for his account of Thomas Lincoln's arrival in Indiana and life in a "half-faced camp." Whatever Thomas did on his arrival in Indiana, he had never lived in a "half-faced camp" before. In each instance when he had migrated from one part of Kentucky to another, in various seasons, he had set about building a cabin for his family. Whether Herndon embellished on Dennis's story or Dennis embellished his own story is not clear. What is clear is that Abraham Lincoln clears up much of the question of what happened that winter in 1816. In a biographical sketch written for John Locke Scripps, Lincoln wrote:

From this place [Kentucky] he [Abraham Lincoln] removed to what is now Spencer County, Indiana, in the autumn of 1816, Abraham then being in his eighth year. ... A few days before completion of his eighth year, in the absence of his father, a flock of wild turkeys approached the *new log cabin* [emphasis added], and Abraham with a rifle-gun, standing inside, shot through a crack and killed one of them.

Watercolor lithograph of the Indiana cabin by John B. Rowbotham for Joseph H. Barrett's Life of Lincoln. *Rowbotham visited Lincoln sites in Kentucky and Indiana in search of Lincoln cabins.* Lincoln National Life Foundation.

The incident described by Lincoln occurred after the family had been in Indiana just under two months and were living in a "new log cabin." John Hanks, Lincoln's second cousin and the man who would help build the Lincoln cabin at Goosenest Prairie near Charleston, Illinois, in 1830, stated that it took all of four days to construct the cabin. This should put to rest the claim of a "half-faced camp" that found the Lincoln family living in it for a full year while their cabin was being built.

Cabin building on the American frontier was standard. Most cabin homes looked similar in overall respects. Sixteen logs one foot in diameter and twenty feet long were selected; eight for the front and eight for the back. Sixteen logs one foot in diameter and eighteen feet long were selected for the end walls. Shorter logs were used to fill in the gables and patch around doors and windows. A total of forty logs were usually required.

While none of the original Kentucky cabins of Thomas Lincoln survived physically, or even through photographs, the Indiana cabin of the Lincolns is believed to have been sketched and photographed. In summer 1864, during Lincoln's reelection campaign, John B. Rowbotham was sent to Kentucky and Indiana by a Cincinnati publisher to locate and sketch the various cabin homes of the Lincolns for use in a Lincoln biography by Joseph H. Barrett. While finding the birth cabin in Kentucky gone, Rowbotham was able to locate the Lincoln cabin near Gentryville, Indiana, and sketch it. As an artist, Rowbotham was a keen observer and had a reputation as a careful researcher. Making his way to Gentryville, Rowbotham interviewed several people still living in the area who were familiar with the Lincoln family and their home. A year later, Rowbotham wrote to William Herndon in response to a letter Herndon wrote to him. "The house lies a little off the Gentryville road on rising ground & is the most perfect reminiscence of Mr L's early life ... Mrs. Lincoln died here & is buried on the summit of a thickly wooded hill about a quarter of a mile & immediately opposite the house." [June 24, 1865]

Since Rowbotham's initial discovery and sketching of the Indiana cabin, two photographs have emerged. The first shows six people posing in front of the Lincoln's Indiana cabin and is purported to have been taken "a few days after Lincoln was assassinated." The second photograph shows the same cabin with two men posing in front of it with a person standing in the doorway. The roof extension and four posts have been removed, but the door and window placements and chimney are in the same location in both photographs and in the Rowbotham watercolor lithograph. A second cabin can be seen in both photographs to the left of the main cabin. According to Jill York O'Bright, Regional Historian, Midwest Region, the right-hand cabin was begun by Thomas and Abraham Lincoln but finished by others when the Lincolns pulled up stakes and migrated to Illinois. It is the left-hand cabin that is believed to be the original Lincoln cabin. It disappeared under unknown circumstances while the right-hand cabin was disassembled and sent to Cincinnati for

display. It too disappeared. Today, the sketch by Rowbotham and the two photographs seen here are the only representations of Thomas Lincoln's Indiana home.

An artist's rendition of the Indiana cabin believed to be based on an early photograph. From a postcard.

The Lincoln cabin, date unknown. From a postcard.

Local residents of Dale, Indiana, posing in front of the Lincoln cabin shortly after Lincoln's assassination. From a postcard.

The Homesite

The Indiana Lincoln Union originally decided that a replica cabin located on the exact site of the original cabin would be inappropriate. Instead, they decided to outline the dimensions of the cabin and fireplace with bronze sill logs and hearth-stones.

Lincoln Park supervisor Horace Weber, who was in charge of the Civilian Conservation Corps crew that uncovered the original hearth-stones of the Lincoln cabin, inspects the excavation site of the stones. A total of 300 stones arranged in three layers were uncovered in 1934.

Photograph by O.V. Brown. The Indiana Lincoln Memorial. A Report of the Indiana Lincoln Union, 1938.

The fireplace is eight feet wide, four feet deep, and rises two feet above the ground.

The bronze sill and fireplace marking the original site of the Lincoln cabin at the Lincoln Boyhood National Memorial. The bronze memorial sits within an enclosure that is one foot below the surrounding level and set off by a stone wall. The memorial sits at the original level of the cabin.

Little Pigeon Creek Community, Spenser County, Indiana

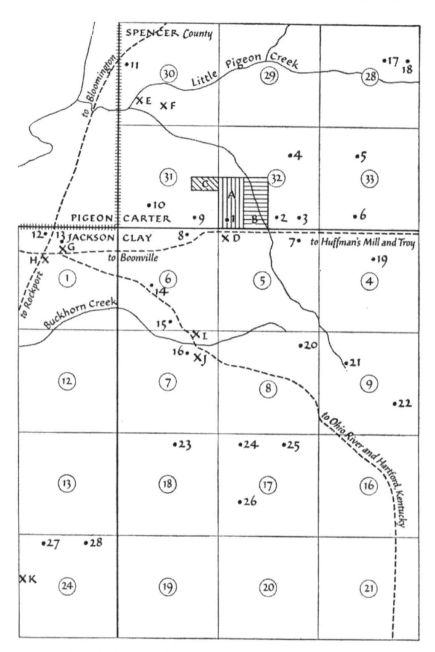

The cabin of Thomas Lincoln (number 1 on map opposite). From a watercolor sketch by James Rowbotham made in 1865. Postcard, ca. 1950.

The Lincoln farm as it appeared in 1895. From Clifford M. Nichols, *Life of Lincoln* (New York, New York: Mast, Crowell & Kirkpatrick, 1896).

Stone marker (placed in 1917) showing the actual location site of the Thomas Lincoln cabin in the schoolyard of the Lincoln City School. Photograph dated 1927. From A Report of the Indiana Lincoln Union, 1938.

THE INDIANA FARM OF THOMAS LINCOLN

Section map showing the Little Pigeon Creek Community along with the farm of Thomas Lincoln (hatched area) and his neighbors (numbers 2-28). Lincoln initially purchased a quarter section consisting of one hundred and sixty acres in the southwest quarter of section 32 (marked A and B). He later purchased twenty acres (C) in section 31 from his neighbor David Casebier, bringing his total to one hundred and eighty acres. He later relinquished eighty acres (the area marked B) to pay off his mortgage. The site of the Lincoln cabin is indicated by the number 1, while Dennis Hanks lived at the site indicated by the number 2. A total of twenty-eight families lived within the area displayed on the map. The Little Pigeon Creek Baptist Church and graveyard where Sarah Lincoln Grigsby is buried is located at the point marked XI just inside the border between sections 6 and 7.

From Louis A. Warren, *Lincoln's Youth. Indiana Years. Seven to Twenty-one, 1816-1830* (New York: Appleton-Century-Crofts, Inc., 1959).

Home of David Turnham (number 4 on map). Turnham was a nearby neighbor of Thomas Lincoln. Postcard, ca. 1959.

The Little Pigeon Creek Baptist Church

A reconstruction of the Little Pigeon Creek Baptist Church located at Rockport, Indiana. From a postcard, ca. 1950.

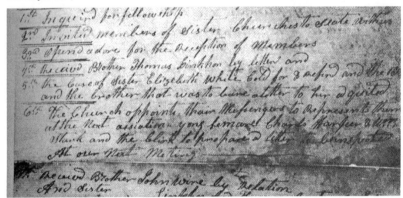

Page from the Little Creek Baptist Church Minute Book with entry showing the admission of Thomas Lincoln as a member. Entry reads: 4th [June] Received Brother Thomas Linkhorn by letter.

On June 22, 1943, the trustees of the church agreed to sell the church's original minute book to Hilbert Bennett of Rockport, Indiana, for one thousand dollars. The money was used to repair and maintain the church facility. The deerskin-covered book held the church's records between its founding in 1816 and 1840. Included among the records were the names of those who joined the church and their baptism, marriage, and death dates as well as records of trial summaries of those members brought before the church council for various alleged offenses. The names of Thomas Lincoln, Sarah Bush Lincoln, and Sarah Lincoln Grigsby appear numerous times in the old book. Photographs from Bess V. Ehrmann, "Old Pigeon Creek Minute Book Sold," Lincoln Herald, vol. 45, no.4 (December 1943).

Organized in 1816, the community of Little Pigeon Creek did not construct a church building until 1821. After several false starts, the congregation appointed a building committee, appointing Thomas Lincoln to oversee construction of a church building even though he and his wife Sarah had not transferred their membership to the church at the time. Not until June 4, 1823, did Thomas "Linkhorn" (Lincoln) become a member of the congregation "by letter" transferring from the Little Mount Separate Baptist Church in Kentucky. Sarah Lincoln joined the church on April 8, 1826, three years after Thomas. Abraham Lincoln chose not to join the church and never did become a member of any church during his lifetime.

Abraham's Sister
Sarah Lincoln
1807-1828

Sarah Lincoln was the first child born to Thomas and Nancy Lincoln while living in the Elizabethtown cabin. Two years older than her brother Abraham, born in 1809, there is no known description of her. Surely Sarah played a role in keeping house, assisting her mother in daily chores. When her mother died in 1818, Sarah, now eleven years old, must have assumed many of the housekeeping duties of her mother.

On August 2, 1826, at age nineteen, Sarah Lincoln married Aaron Grigsby in the Little Pigeon Creek Baptist Church. A year and a half later, just shy of her twenty-first birthday, Sarah died giving birth to a stillborn son. She was buried in the cemetery of the Little Pigeon Creek Baptist Church where three years later her husband was laid to rest beside her.

It was the second great tragedy of the young Abraham Lincoln's life. Devastated by the death of his sister, Lincoln blamed Aaron for not seeking medical attention soon enough, thereby contributing to Sarah's death. The grievance resulted in a split between the two families up to the time of Thomas Lincoln's departure for Illinois in 1830.

Top: Little Pigeon Creek Baptist Church, 1986.

Middle: *Little Pigeon Creek Baptist Church burial ground located behind the church building. The cemetery was laid out in 1825 and the first burial occurred in 1826. There are over four hundred graves in the cemetery. The graves of Sarah Lincoln Grigsby and her husband Aaron Grigsby are located to the left of center between the two trees.*

Bottom: *The gravestones of Aaron Grigsby (left) and Sarah Lincoln Grigsby (right). The markers read:*

AARON	SARAH LINCOLN
GRIGSBY	WIFE OF
BORN	AARON GRIGSBY
1801	FEB. 10, 1807
DIED	JAN. 20, 1828
1831	

Men show by what they worship, what they are.

Report of the Indiana Lincoln Union, 1938

On February 19, 1962, President John F. Kennedy signed an act establishing the Lincoln Boyhood National Memorial. The act authorized the transfer of the state of Indiana's Lincoln State Park and Nancy Hanks Lincoln Memorial to the National Park Service. Up until that time the farm and cabin site of Thomas Lincoln and the grave of Nancy Hanks Lincoln had been under the stewardship of the Indiana Department of Conservation, Division of State Parks, Lands and Waters.

Efforts to memorialize the Lincoln Indiana home and the Nancy Hanks Lincoln grave go back to the early 1870s when a group of local citizens formed a committee to raise funds to obtain a suitable marker to mark the grave of Lincoln's mother. The project was initially abandoned for lack of funds. Several subsequent efforts were initiated over the next several years, culminating in the purchase of sixteen acres surrounding the gravesite by the Spencer County Commission who then transferred the property to the state with the stipulation that the property would revert back to the county if not properly maintained. By 1906, the property was in a state of disrepair and the Indiana general assembly established a Board of Commissioners to oversee the site and the establishment of a suitable memorial.

In 1917, efforts were begun to locate the exact site of the Lincoln cabin, which proved successful. Drawing on local residents' memories, including two individuals who were alive at the time the Lincolns lived in the cabin, the site was located and confirmed by locating several original hearthstones and other household artifacts. A stone marker (below) was placed on a spot determined to be the center of the cabin.

In 1923, the Indiana state legislature created the Lincoln Memorial Commission and placed control of the gravesite under the State Department of Conservation. Several organizations and patriotic groups supported the establishment of a memorial and offered their help. In 1926, the Indiana Lincoln Union was formed to assist the state in its effort and raised $229,000 toward building a memorial. The Lincoln Memorial Commission then purchased the forty-six acre Patmore farm, which included the cabin site. With the transfer to the state of the sixteen acres containing the gravesite owned by the county, the Lincoln Memorial Commission now owned a total of sixty-two acres.

Indiana moved forward in earnest to build a suitable memorial to Abraham Lincoln and his mother Nancy Hanks Lincoln. On January 24, 1927, the state hired the renowned landscape architect Frederick Law Olmstead to prepare a preliminary design for the memorial park. Using Olmstead's design, the state went to work. Over the next ten years it removed several buildings from the site, relocated Highway 162, graded the area, began a program of reforestation (57,000 trees and 3,200 shrubs) and began building the plaza and parking facilities. Next came the walking "Trail of Twelve Stones" commemorating Lincoln's life.

In 1933, the Civilian Conservation Corps, while excavating the cabin site, uncovered the original hearthstones, later used to make the bronze casting of the fireplace used in the cabin memorial.

On December 10, 1940, work began on the memorial building. The final design consisted of three architectural units, a central cloister connecting two memorial halls located at opposite ends of the building. Set into the curved walls of the cloister are five limestone panels thirteen feet long by eight feet high depicting important periods in Lincoln's life.

Although construction was completed in 1944, the formal dedication of the building was postponed until the end of the Second World War. Unfortunately, there is no record that a formal dedication ever occurred. In 1966, the National Park Service, following their assumption of the site, added a Visitor Center to the cloister section of the building.

Photograph by O.V. Brown. The Indiana Lincoln Memorial. A Report of the Indiana Lincoln Union, 1938.

SPENCER COUNTY
MEMORIAL
to
ABRAHAM LINCOLN
WHO LIVED
ON THIS SPOT
FROM
1816 — 1830

Lincoln Boyhood National Memorial

The Trail of Twelve Stones

In 1931 the Indiana Lincoln Union planned a walking trail of twelve stones recovered from various Lincoln sites. Each of the stones memorializes an important episode in Lincoln's life. The trail winds for one mile through the historic site.

1. A stone from the Sinking Spring birthplace site.

2. Stone marker from the monument erected on the cabin site in 1917.

3. A stone from the store at Jonesboro where Lincoln worked as a clerk.

4. A stone from the Western Sun and Commercial Advertiser *building in Vincennes, Indiana.*

5. A foundation stone from the Lincoln- Berry store in New Salem, Illinois.

6. Four bricks from Mary Todd's girlhood home in Lexington, Kentucky.

7. A stone from the White House.

8. A stone from the Anderson Cottage located at Soldiers' Home in Washington, D.C.

9. A boulder from the Gettysburg Battlefield in Gettysburg, Pennsylvania.

10. A stone from the Old Capitol building in Washington, D.C.

11. A portion of the sandstone column from the Petersen House where Lincoln died.

12. The Culver Stone taken from the Lincoln tomb in Springfield, Illinois, and used to create a gravesite marker for Nancy Hanks Lincoln.

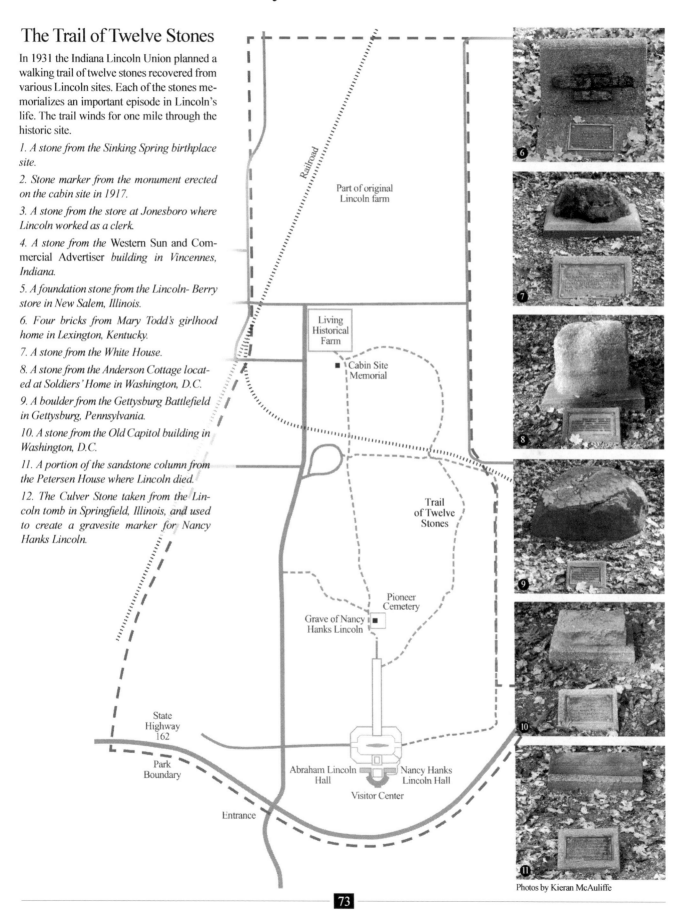

Photos by Kieran McAuliffe

All is a dense forest – wild and grand.
William H. Herndon

No headboard – no footboard to mark the Spot where Abm Lincoln's Mother lies – Curious – and unaccountable is it not?

Lincoln Farm   Septr 14th 1865
Started [out] to find Mrs Lincoln's grave – it is on a Knob – hill or Knowl about ½ m S.E. of the Lincoln house – passed out of the lane going East – landed at the grave – tied my horse: the grave was – is on the very top or crown of the hill. The Know or Knowl is a heavy timbered one. A Space is cut out of the forest by felling the trees Somewhat circularly. In the centre of this Small cleared place about 15 feet from a large white oak tree – rather Somewhat between 2 of them, lies buried Mrs Lincoln. God bless her if I could breathe life into her again I would do it. Could I only whisper in her Ear – "Your son was Presdt – of the U.S. from 1861 to 1866 [sic]," I would be satisfied. I have heard much of this blessed, good woman. I stood bare headed in reverence at her grave. I can't Say why – yet I felt in the presence of the living woman translated to another world. "God bless her," said her Son to me once and I repeat that which
    Echoes audibly in my soul – "God bless her."
The grave is almost undistinguishable: it has Sunk down, leaving a Kind of hollow. There is no fence around the graveyard and no tomb – no head board to mark where She lies. At her head – close to it I peeled a dog wood bush and cut or marked my name on it. Mrs Lincoln is buried between two or more persons – Said to be Hall & his wife [Levi Hall and Nancy Hanks Hall, the sister of Lucy Hanks, Lincoln's grandmother] on the one hand and Some Children on her left hand – There are two hollows or sinks. Nat Grigsby & Richardson were with me at the time – they said this was *the* grave. ... After looking at the grave and Contemplating in Silence the mutations of things – death – immortality – God, I left, I hope, the grave, a better man – at least if but for one moment.

From Douglas L. Wilson and Rodney O. Davis, *Herndon's Informants* (Chicago, IL: University of Illinois Press, 1998) 116.

Nancy Hanks
By Rosemary Benet

If Nancy Hanks
Came back as a ghost,
Seeking news
Of what she loved most,
She'd ask first
"Where's my son?
What's happened to Abe?
What's he done?"

"Poor little Abe,
Left all alone
Except for Tom,
Who's a rolling stone;
He was only nine
The year I died.
I remember still
How hard he cried."

"Scraping along
In a little shack,
With hardly a shirt
To cover his back,
And a prairie wind
To blow him down,
Or pinching times
If he went to town."

"You wouldn't know
About my son?
Did he grow tall?
Did he have fun?
Did he learn to read?
Did he get to town?
Do you know his name?
Did he get on?"

Nancy Hanks Lincoln Grave

Tombstone marking the grave of Nancy Hanks Lincoln.
The stone was provided by Clement Studebaker in 1879,
sixty-one years after Nancy Lincoln's death.

The inscription reads:

NANCY HANKS
LINCOLN
Mother of President
LINCOLN
DIED
Oct. 5 A.D. 1818
Aged 35 Years
Erected by a Friend of her martyred son
1879

The "Culver Stone."
In 1902 sculptor J.S. Culver obtained a discarded stone
from Abraham Lincoln's original monument in Springfield,
Illinois, and sculpted a memorial stone for Nancy Hanks Lincoln.
The stone was originally placed in front of the Studebaker
gravestone, but was later moved to a point along
the Trail of Twelve Stones.

The inscription on the bronze plaque reads:

IN MEMORIAM
THIS STONE FROM LINCOLN'S
TOMB IN SPRINGFIELD
ILLINOIS WAS PRESENTED BY A GRATEFUL PEOPLE
IN TRIBUTE TO HIS MOTHER

The Milk Sickness

In this sad world of ours, sorrow comes to all; and to the young,
it comes with bitterest agony, because it takes them unawares.

Abraham Lincoln, letter to Fanny McCullough, December 23, 1862.

In the nineteenth century many diseases were not understood. This was especially true of infectious diseases caused by microbes. Often ascribed to "bad air" or an imbalance of "humors," disease had as many explanations as there were people it seemed. Among the numerous diseases that plagued the early settlers in certain states was a strange malady known as "the milk sick" or "milk sickness." The disease was most prevalent in the states of Kentucky, Indiana, Illinois, and Ohio, and was believed to come from the dairy and meat products of cattle that had eaten a plant commonly referred to as "snakeroot." Unknown at the time but discovered years later, the plant (formerly known as Eupatorium rugosum and now reclassified as Ageratina altissima) produces a chemical compound now identified as "tremetol," also known as "tremetone." Tremetol acts as a neurotoxin, which once ingested in sufficient quantity, causes death.

In the fall of 1818, Abraham Lincoln's mother, Nancy Hanks Lincoln, apparently contracted the disease and died after a week of illness. While Nancy Lincoln's symptoms were never described, the disease results in anorexia, severe vomiting (giving rise to the term puking sickness), constipation, extreme thirst without appetite, inability to sleep, and in severe cases coma followed by death. One of the standard treatments of the disease was the standard frontier dose of brandy and honey. Brandy, it was thought, was an antidote for poison in general.

Snakeroot grows in the shaded areas of woodland where it grows to as much as three feet in height, showing clusters of small fuzzy white flower heads composed of tiny white blossoms. During dry spells when pastureland becomes depleted of forage, cattle move into adjoining wooded areas where the plant thrives and is eaten by the cattle in place of grass. The cattle become "infected" with the toxin that makes its way undigested into the animal's tissues and milk.

The disease appeared in the Little Pigeon Creek community in September 1818, when Nancy Lincoln's brother-in-law, Thomas Sparrow, came down with the symptoms. Anticipating his death, Thomas Sparrow made out his will, leaving all his meager assets to his wife Elizabeth. Nancy Lincoln appears as a witness on the will, showing Nancy was in good health at the time. Within a week of making his will, Thomas Sparrow was dead, and his wife soon contracted the disease and died within the week. A third neighbor, Mrs. Peter Brooner, became ill and died. Nancy nursed Mrs.

Brooner during her illness and soon developed the symptoms herself, dying on October 5, 1818.

At the time of Nancy Lincoln's death there were four other individuals living in the Lincoln cabin in addition to Nancy: her husband, Thomas, her children Sarah, age eleven, and Abraham, age nine, and Dennis Hanks, her nineteen-year-old cousin.

In 1865, Dennis wrote to Lincoln's law partner and close friend, William Herndon, describing Nancy Lincoln's death.

Mrs Lincoln was taken sick with what is known as the milk sickness; she struggled on day by day, a good Christian woman, and died on the seventh day after she was taken sick. She knew she was going to die and called her children to her dying side and told them to be good and kind to their father, to one another, and to the world, expressing a hope that they might live as they had been taught by her to love men, reverence and worship God.

Despite the belief that the scourge of what pioneers called the "milk sickness" was caused by cattle eating snakeroot, it seems unlikely that the children of the Lincoln cabin somehow remained immune to the poison even though as children they most likely consumed substantial amounts of the milk on a daily basis from tainted cows. A potent neurological toxin would hardly pass over the children and father and kill only the mother. Tremetol appears to be an all or nothing toxin whose effect is almost always lethal. On the other hand, a bacterial infection common to cattle known as Brucellosis also infects individuals through ingesting milk and meat from infected cattle. As is common with infectious disease, not everyone exposed to the agent contracts it or develops symptoms. It is more likely that the other members of the Lincoln cabin, while exposed to the disease of Brucellosis, were able to ward off its effect while Nancy Lincoln was not.

While we may never know the true cause of Nancy Lincoln's death, the effect of her passing was devastating to the two young children and their father. For the next year, the family slowly slipped into a degraded state, suffering from the lack of Nancy Lincoln's kind and caring hand in keeping the family and cabin in a proper state. Thomas Lincoln, realizing the poor state of his family, decided to find a wife and mother to rectify the situation that was growing desperate.

Ageratina altissima (formerly Eupatorium rugosum),
more commonly known as Snakeroot.

Pioneer Cemetery

The pioneer cemetery and gravestone of Nancy Hanks Lincoln. Buried alongside her grave are her sister and brother-in-law, Elizabeth Hanks Sparrow and Thomas Sparrow. All three died within a few days of one another, allegedly from the "milk sickness."

The burial of Nancy Hanks Lincoln depicted in a diorama located in the Nancy Hanks Lincoln Hall at the Visitor Center, Lincoln Boyhood National Memorial.

The Memorial Building

In deciding to build an appropriate memorial building for the park site, consideration was given to the building's size and location. Paramount to considering the placement of the building was the concern that it not cause an "imposition" on the "humble gravesite" of Nancy Hanks Lincoln. The building and its location above all must be "in harmony with the *spiritus loci.*" The original architectural proposal included a building of massive size with a 150-foot tower dominating the landscape, which was anything but in harmony with the simple grave of Lincoln's mother.

Rejecting the original proposal, the Indiana Department of Conservation, together with the Indiana Lincoln Union, decided on a simple structure containing "a central memorial feature, a small hall suitable for public meetings, and a large room with simple facilities for the comfort of visitors." Included in the final design was a semicircular wall displaying large, sculpted panels weighing ten tons each and measuring eight feet tall by thirteen and one-half feet wide. After long delays and considerable debate, the Department of

The Indiana Panel: 1816-1830. The Boyhood Days of Lincoln. *The Indiana Lincoln Union hired Indiana sculptor Elmer H. Daniels to provide five large panels for the semi-circular wall of the connecting cloister depicting important events of Lincoln's life. Daniels chose "Labor" for the Indiana panel.*

The Memorial Visitor Center building consists of two small buildings, called "halls" joined by a semi-circular cloister whose outer wall supports the five sculptured panels depicting events in Abraham Lincoln's life. The two halls appear identical on the exterior, but differ interiorly. In 1966, three years after taking over the Indiana site, the National Park Service added the Visitor Center to the rear of the cloister between the two halls.

Conservation hired Elmer H. Daniels to sculpt the building's panels. Five panels were chosen, depicting five phases of Abraham Lincoln's life: Kentucky, Indiana, Illinois, Washington, and a central panel designated "And Now He Belongs to the Ages."

The construction contract was awarded to the W.A. Armstrong company of Terre Haute, Indiana, and ground was broken on December 10, 1940. By 1943 the work was complete and dedication of the building with its massive panels was scheduled for early 1944, only to be postponed until the end of World War II. A formal dedication of the building, however, never took place.

In 1959, a proposal to place the Indiana site within the Federal Park System began a series of studies and debates ending with President John F. Kennedy signing the act authorizing the establishment of the Lincoln Boyhood National Memorial within the National Park System on February 19, 1962. The formal dedication ceremony, delayed since 1944, took place on July 10, 1962.

The Nancy Hanks Lincoln Hall.
Fireplace located in the Nancy Hanks Lincoln Hall located to the left of the cloister. The hall serves as a lounge suitable for meetings and receptions.

The Abraham Lincoln Hall.
Located to the right of the cloister, the hall measures thirty by sixty feet and holds 250 people in pew-like seats. A speaker's rostrum is located at the front of the hall and a balcony is located in the rear.

On to Illinois 1830

In the autumn of 1829, Thomas Lincoln decided to move once again. His son, Abraham, was now a grown man. This time Thomas picked the fertile plains of Illinois. John Hanks had settled four years earlier in Macon County, Illinois, and sent back glowing reports of the new land. The milk sickness had made another return to southern Indiana and must have made an impact on the family that had suffered once before from it. Thomas and Sarah sold Sarah's lot in Elizabethtown for one hundred and twenty-three dollars and eighty of their Indiana acres, which they now owned outright, to James Gentry. Thomas also sold off his livestock and bought four stout oxen and a large wagon for the trip north.

As part of their preparations, Thomas and Sarah also secured a letter of "dismission" from their church to take to their new church in Illinois. The letter was withdrawn, however, over the protests of Nancy Grigsby (Sarah Lincoln Grigsby's mother-in-law) who was still festering over Abraham's anger about his sister's death. The letter was eventually reissued, however, a month after it had been withdrawn, suggesting that whatever differences existed were now resolved.

Before leaving Kentucky in 1816, the young boy Abraham had been taken by his mother to visit the grave of the baby Tommy Lincoln. Now, before leaving Indiana, the grown Abraham paid a last visit with his stepmother to the grave of his birth mother. Saying their goodbyes, the three Lincolns together with the Johnston, Hanks and Hall families hitched up three wagons, two drawn by two sets of oxen, the third by horses, and started out on the long wintery trek northward into Illinois. It was the first day of March in the year 1830. Abraham Lincoln had just passed his twenty-first birthday and was, by law, his own man. As the party made its way toward Vincennes and the Wabash River, Abraham began to think of his own future and what lay ahead in a new and strange state. He wondered whether it would bode ill or good. Only time would tell.

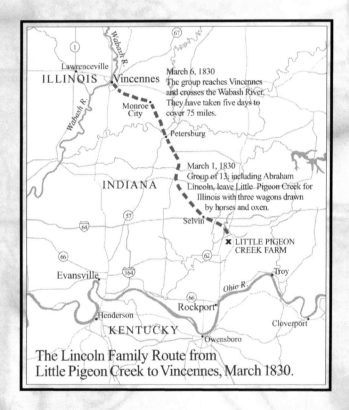

March 6, 1830
The group reaches Vincennes and crosses the Wabash River. They have taken five days to cover 75 miles.

March 1, 1830
Group of 13, including Abraham Lincoln, leave Little Pigeon Creek for Illinois with three wagons drawn by horses and oxen.

The Lincoln Family Route from Little Pigeon Creek to Vincennes, March 1830.

Lincoln Trail State Memorial

The Lincoln caravan crossed the Wabash River into Illinois at a point where the Lincoln Memorial Bridge now stands. Located on the Illinois side is the Lincoln Trail State Memorial. The memorial was created by Nellie Verne Walker and erected by the Illinois Daughters of the American Revolution in 1938 to commemorate Abraham Lincoln's passage into Illinois. Standing out from the large marble panel is an heroic bronze statue of the twenty-one-year-old Lincoln walking alongside one of the ox-drawn wagons that accompanied the caravan. Carved above Lincoln on the marble panel is the figure of a woman, the *Spirit of Destiny*, whose outstretched arm guides the Lincolns to their new home. The monument depicts only a part of the caravan that consisted of thirteen people, two ox-drawn wagons, and one horse-drawn wagon. The caravan crossed over the river into Illinois on March 6, 1830.

The inscription on the base of the monument reads:
IN THE LATE WINTER OF 1830, A FEW WEEKS AFTER HIS 21st BIRTHDAY,
ABRAHAM LINCOLN PASSED THIS WAY WITH HIS FATHER'S FAMILY,
ENTERING THE STATE OF ILLINOIS FOR THE FIRST TIME.

Acknowledgements

As every author well knows, it takes a village to write a book. This work is no exception. We are indebted to many individuals for their generous help in bringing this publication to life. First among these is Celia Lynn McAuliffe. We thank her for her exceptional editorial skills. Her keen eye has proven invaluable in turning a rough manuscript into a more polished narrative. We also thank Joseph E. Garrera, Executive Director of the Lehigh Valley Heritage Museum in Allentown, Pennsylvania, for his many helpful suggestions and encouragement. We thank our good friend Lincoln artist and historian Lloyd Ostendorf (deceased) for allowing us to use his fine portrait of Nancy Hanks. We also wish to thank Joan Chaconas, History Specialist, Surratt House Museum. We would be remiss not to recognize the significant contributions to our understanding of Lincoln's early years of William E. Barton, Louis A. Warren, and R. Gerald McMurtry – three of the early giants of Lincoln scholarship. And lastly, all the wonderful people along the Lincoln Trail who generously provided their help and knowledge. We thank you all.

Selected Sources

Preface

R. Vincent Enlow, *The Abraham Lincoln Genesis Cover-up: The Censored Origins of an Illustrious Ancestor* (New Providence, N.J.; Genealogy Today Publications, 2001), 2.

KENTUCKY: The Birthplace

William E. Barton, *The Lincolns in Their Old Kentucky Home: An address delivered before the Filson Club, Louisville, Kentucky*, December 4, 1922 (Berea, Kentucky: Berea College Press, 1923).

Louis A. Warren, *Lincoln's Parentage and Childhood* (New York, NY: The Century Company, 1926).

Mabel Kunkle, *Abraham Lincoln: Unforgettable American* (Charlotte, North Carolina: The Delmar Company, 1976).

The Birthplace Cabin: Fact or Fiction?

Louis A. Warren, "Lincoln's Mythical Childhood Homes," *The Lincoln Kinsman*, vol. 30 (December 1940).

Roy Hayes, "Is the Lincoln Birthplace Cabin Authentic?," *Abraham Lincoln Quarterly*, vol. 5, no. 3 (September 1948), 129.

Louis A. Warren, "The Authenticity of Lincoln's Birthplace Cabin: The Jacob S. Brothers Tradition," *Lincoln Lore*, No. 1016 (September 27, 1948).

Louis A. Warren, "The Authenticity of Lincoln's Birthplace Cabin: The John A. Davenport Tradition," *Lincoln Lore*, No.1019 (October 18, 1948).

Dwight T. Pitcaithley, "Abraham Lincoln's Birthplace Cabin: The Making of an American Icon," in *Myth, Memory, and the Making of the American Landscape*, ed. Paul A. Shackel (Gainesville, FL: University Press of Florida, 2001), 250.

Douglas L. Wilson and Rodney O. Davis, *Herndon's Informants* (Chicago, IL: University of Illinois Press, 1998).

Knob Creek: The Boyhood Home

Louis A. Warren, *Lincoln's Parentage and Childhood* (New York, NY: The Century Company, 1926).

R. Gerald McMurtry, "Re-discovering the Supposed Grave of Lincoln's Brother," *Lincoln Herald*, vol. 48, no. 1 (February 1946), 12-19.

Nancy Hanks

Nancy Hanks Commission Report to the Governor, Papers of William G. Connelly, Cultural Center, Charleston, West Virginia, September 29, 1925.

Louis A. Warren, *Lincoln's Parentage and Childhood* (New York, NY: The Century Company, 1926).

William E. Barton, *The Lineage of Lincoln* (Indianapolis, IN: Bobbs-Merrill, 1929).

Louis A. Warren, *The Lincoln Kinsman.* "The Richard Berry Family", No. 16 (October 1939).

Paul H. Verduin, "Lincoln, the Hankses, and the American Revolution: New Research, New Light," *The Lincoln Newsletter*, Spring 1992.

INDIANA: The Formative Years

David A. Kimball, "The Lincoln Boyhood National Memorial," *Lincoln Herald*, vol. 66, no. 1 (Spring 1964), 15-18.

Adin Baber, "The Lincoln Log Cabins," *Lincoln Herald*, vol. 71, no. 1 (Spring 1969), 19-26.

Jill York O'Bright, "There I Grew Up...": A History of the Administration of Abraham Lincoln's Boyhood Home," (National Park Service, 1987).

Joe Grove, "Lincoln's Stepmother: The Discovery of a Sarah Lincoln Photograph," *The Rail Splitter*, vol. 8 no. 3 (Winter 2003).

Books By Edward Steers, Jr.

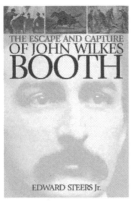

The Escape and
Capture of
John Wilkes Booth

His Name
Is Still Mudd

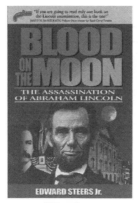

Blood on
the Moon

Lincoln
Legends

Hoax

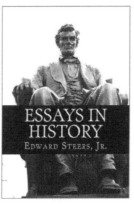

Essays
in History

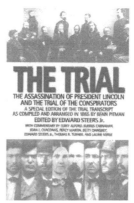

The Trial

Lincoln's
Assassination

Port Hudson
to Cedar Creek

Don't You Know
There's a War On?

I'll Be
Seeing You

Der Tagebuch
The Journal

Maps By Kieran McAuliffe

 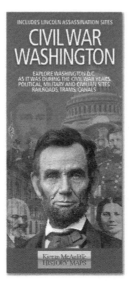 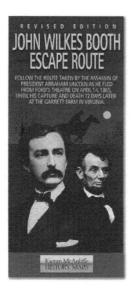 

Folded map measures 5 by 11 inches.

Abraham Lincoln Map   ISBN-13: 978-0986894503

A unique detailed map showing the life of Abraham Lincoln from his birth in Kentucky to his departure from Springfield, Illinois, as President-elect. Every part of his life is covered, including his youth, his life in New Salem, his part in the Black Hawk War, his life in Springfield, and his legal and political career – from state legislator to U.S. congressman, to his attempt for the U.S. Senate and the Lincoln-Douglas Debates, and two years later, to his election as President of the United States. Extensive chronology details the life of Lincoln along with important events in American history.
48 pictures and 3 inset maps. Reading list.

Civil War Washington   ISBN-13: 978-0986894510

Explore Washington, D.C., as it was during the Civil War years. This map shows political, military and civilian sites, railroads, trams, and canals, and sites connected to the assassination of Abraham Lincoln. Detailed index and grid helps you find what you are looking for. Many sites connected to the President are detailed. An introduction to the system of forts that surrounded the city is included.
Over 60 photos. Reading list.

John Wilkes Booth Escape Route Map   ISBN-13: 978-0986894534

Follow the route taken by the assassin of President Abraham Lincoln as he fled from Ford's Theatre on April 14, 1865, until his capture and death 12 days later at the Garrett Farm in Virginia. Completely updated inside and out. Presenting the latest research into the escape attempt of John Wilkes Booth after he assassinated President Abraham Lincoln. Booth's escape route and the search routes are clearly shown and color coded. Follow the fugitives and the soldiers day by day, hour by hour. A 1200-word commentary details the assassination, the escape, and the capture and death of Booth.
34 pictures and illustrations. Reading list.

Raid on Richmond   ISBN-13: 978-0986894527

The incredible story of the Kilpatrick-Dahlgren Raid features all the elements of a Hollywood thriller. Starring Judson Kilpatrick – a cocky West Point graduate and cavalry officer, and Ulric Dahlgren – a dashing blue-blood staff officer who had lost his lower right leg just months before during the Gettysburg campaign. Add a dark and stormy night, a planned but failed prison break, a hanging, an ambush in the dark, a missing corpse, and handwritten notes detailing the destruction of Richmond and the murder of Jefferson Davis and the Confederate Cabinet. A 1200-word commentary details the raid that might have led to the assassination of Abraham Lincoln.
34 pictures and illustrations. Reading list.

Notes

Made in the USA
Lexington, KY
12 July 2019